LUDWIG'S
HAN[DBOOK]

of Old Testament Rulers & Cities

CHARLES LUDWIG

ACCENT BOOKS
Denver, Colorado

ACCENT BOOKS

A division of Accent Publications, Inc.
12100 W. Sixth Avenue
P. O. Box 15337
Denver, Colorado 80215

Library of Congress Catalog Card Number 84-070426
ISBN 0-89636-130-6

In memory of
Albert J. Kempin

He helped
keep the candles burning!

Contents

PREFACE

This book is not a revised Ph.D. thesis. Nor is it a textbook slanted toward graduate students in archaeology. Rather, it's a plain book in simple language which attempts to present a glimpse of the years before and during Old Testament times by viewing some of the highlights.

As in the companion volume, *Ludwig's Handbook of New Testament Rulers & Cities*, we have studied those years through the eyes of contemporary rulers, and by walking through the streets of such cities as Nineveh, Jericho and Babylon.

Because of archaeology, and the discovery of ancient monuments and scrolls; and because we can now read cuneiform and hieroglyphics, startling new dimensions have been given to ancient writings. These new dimensions help us to see Moses, Joshua, Nebuchadnezzar, Antiochus Epiphanes, and others in a new way. Also, they almost enable us to see—and smell—such now-disappeared cities as Sodom, Babylon, and Nineveh.

The story of the solution to the ancient riddles of cuneiform and hieroglyphics has edge-of-the-seat interest. But now that we know what the pharaohs had for breakfast and what they used for ink, we have many questions. Here are some which the book has tried to answer:

(1) Why did Hatshepsut—thought to be the pharaoh's daughter who rescued Moses from the bulrushes—insist on wearing a golden beard?

(2) Why does the mummy of Rameses II spend such long periods in Paris?

(3) How did Isaiah know that Cyrus would free the Babylonian exiles more than a century before Cyrus was born?

(4) Is it really true, as Edward Gibbon insists, that history is "little more than the register of the crimes, follies, and misfortunes of mankind"? Or can we see the firm hand of God molding the centuries in those faraway years?

(5) Did God ever use wicked men to do His will?

Those past millenniums are filled with interest and they can be most interesting and helpful to us as we study the Old and New Testaments. The months I have spent in writing this book have firmed my faith in Christ.

Charles Ludwig
Tucson, Arizona

Chapter 1

Opened Windows to the Past

Until a little over a century ago almost all of the information available about Old Testament times was found only in the Bible. Scholars were completely unaware of contemporary sources that would confirm—or deny—the stories about rulers and cities and events described by Moses and others.

Yes, there were contemporary stories about the rulers and cities of New Testament times. The histories of the Caesars were readily available. But Old Testament times? Those years were almost completely blank. Scholars shrugged. "We don't know," they said. Today, however, the story is completely different. Now, as the result of what I believe to have been divinely-inspired persistence, vast new knowledge about Old Testament times is readily available. Better yet, the windows that enable us to understand that knowledge have been flung wide.

Would you like to know intimate details about the pharaohs who dominated Egypt? Now we know why they were buried with their mouths slightly ajar, their approximate ages at the time of their deaths, the kind of medicine they used, what they ate, the condition of their teeth—and why they insisted on being buried in pyramids.

We even have hints about some of their romances!

Have you ever cringed at the laws of Moses? An eye for an eye sounds rather severe. If you have you will discover that many of them were mild in comparison to the laws of Hammurabi (also spelled Hammurapi), the bearded ruler who lived half a millennium before Moses was born.

Edward Gibbon declared that history is "little more than the register of the crimes, follies, and misfortunes of mankind." Believers, of course, know better. We know that God has a plan for mankind and that He has often used a pharaoh or other ruthless dictator to help work out His plan. The truth flowing through the opened windows to the past has confirmed that fact, and underlined it.

Opening those formerly bolted windows was mainly accomplished by learning to read hieroglyphics and cuneiform—strange markings that Christian nations had ignored for seventeen hundred years.

Roman emperors and popes had decorated the plazas in Rome with thirteen Egyptian obelisks. But no one was even interested in discussing the possible meaning of the dramatic pictures and symbols that covered them. This is strange, for there had been hints that those indented birds, lines, curves, and triangles had special meaning.

The respected Clement of Alexandria, born in Egypt about A.D. 155, had coined the word: hieroglyphics. He based it on the Greek words for graven image. That word was well known. But the masses were not interested. They were all assured that civilization had started in Greece! Why should they bother with stupid marks carved by the Egyptians when there were gladiator fights to occupy their time?

And just as hieroglyphics were ignored so, too, was the wedge-type writing found on the clay slabs in Mesopotamia ignored. After all, they—the Romans and the Greeks—were civilized!

For centuries, farmers around Mosul on the banks of the Tigris in northern Mesopotamia (now Iraq), occasionally unearthed tablets covered with arrow-headed, pyramid-shaped characters. More concerned, however, with wheat and barley, they paid little attention to these lifeless slabs. Still, they deserved a name.

The natives dubbed them *misimari*—nail writing.

Europeans also shrugged. But like the natives they agreed the baked slabs should be named. Thomas Hyde did them that honor in 1700. He identified them as "cuneiform." Cuneiform comes from the Latin *cuneus* which means wedge. It never occurred to this Englishman that cuneiform could be a form of writing. To him, it was an out-of-date form of Oriental decoration. But as mistaken as he was, he was generous in comparison to the Koran which speaks of "bricks baked in hell and written by demons."

In 1732 Isaac Preston Cory issued a book in London which intrigued a handful of scholars. He wrote: "We are accustomed to regard Hebrew Scriptures and Latin writings as the only records of antiquity. Yet there have been other languages. . . . Where are those from *Assyria* and *Babylonia*?" (Italics mine.)

Cory's book whetted interest throughout Europe in cuneiform, for some suspected that there was a chance—a very slight chance to be sure—that cuneiform might, just might, be a form of writing. Between 1666 and 1681, Jean Chardin went to the East Indies to buy diamonds. On his way back he stopped in Persia, made notes of the strange markings, and published them in a book in 1711.

Half a century after Chardin's book, Carsten Niebuhr, son of a German pastor, decided to have a look. He boarded ship with a Danish expedition headed for Bombay. All the passengers other than himself died of disease or were killed on the way. He survived only through a ruse. He disguised himself as a native. On his return from India, he stopped in Persia, made a few drawings of cuneiform and published them in a book titled *Description of a Voyage to Arabia and Neighboring Lands.*

Niebuhr's illustrations were excellent. He suggested that

11

the three different sets of inscriptions at Persepolis were in three separate languages. Moreover, he was convinced that cuneiform was alphabetic and that it contained forty-two letters. Nonetheless, he was unable to solve the riddle.

Another who tried was Gerhard Tychsen, a noted Hebrew scholar. He agreed that three separate languages had been used; but he disagreed that cuneiform was alphabetic. The paper he published insisted that the lines were phonetic, that each symbol represented a complete syllable, or even an entire word.

Much of Tychsen's work was wrong.

A few years later, Georg Grotefend decided to tackle the problem. He had only a limited education. But he had a passion for puzzles, acrostics, philology—and the Bible. As he concentrated on a copy of the trilingual inscription from Persepolis, he was convinced that somewhere the words, King of Kings, Darius, and Xerxes would be found in each of the languages.

In less than a year this twenty-seven-year-old had made substantial progress. In section one, he had unraveled the lines:

> Darius, great king, the king of kings, the king of countries, the son of Hystaspes, the Achaemenian. . . .

And in section two, he unscrambled the words:

> Xerxes, great king, king of kings, the son of King Darius, the Achaemenian.

On September 4, 1802, Grotefend presented his partial solution to the Gottingen Academy. The wise old men in the academy, however, refused to publish his work or give him any recognition. Why? Because he was not a professional Orientalist!

The next one to have success with cuneiform was Major Rawlinson who was attached to the British Mission in Persia. In 1835, at the age of twenty-five, Rawlinson was challenged by the fact that Grotefend had solved the symbols in king of kings, Darius, and Xerxes. Perhaps, he reasoned, I can find the total solution. At the time, he did not realize the formidable difficulties involved. A major one was that he was stationed at Kirmanshah—on the western frontier of Persia. This isolated spot was many miles from the nearest European library. Also, he did not have the records of those who had labored on the project in previous years. Nonetheless, he set to work.

As Rawlinson bent over his desk, he learned about a set of inscriptions on the face of the sacred rock at Behistun (near the present city of Hamadan in Western Iran). The moment his schedule permitted, he made the tedious trip to the base of the trilingual inscription. Lifting his eyes to the ancient markings which he estimated to be 160 feet above the valley floor, his spine literally tingled.

But how was he to get to it?

Since he could not make accurate copy from the base of the cliff, he hired workers to let him down in a basket over the inscription. This was extremely dangerous, for not only might the rope break, but a trigger-happy native might shoot him for desecrating such a sacred place.

Eventually Rawlinson learned that this was a Darius inscription and that it was written in Old Persian, Elamite, and Babylonian. With this key, plus the aid of a brilliant Irish minister, Edward Hincks, together with the help of Edwin Norris, Secretary of the Royal Asiatic Society, Rawlinson solved most of the problems connected with the understanding of cuneiform. In honor of his efforts, he was knighted, and is now remembered as Sir Henry Creswicke Rawlinson.

The conquest of cuneiform had taken nearly one and a half centuries! The conquest, however, was worthwhile, for it enabled scholars to decipher the many libraries of clay tablets which were in the process of being discovered. But even though cuneiform could now be read, its solution was not a headline event. Then an unknown youth made a startling discovery.

While the American Civil War was fermenting in 1861, twenty-one-year-old George Smith began to spend his lunch hours and evenings in the British Museum. He was especially drawn to the large collection of clay tablets on which cuneiform symbols had been recorded. Noticing his intense interest, Samuel Birch, Keeper of the Museum, began a quiet investigation. He soon learned that because of lack of funds, Smith had been unable to attend a university. As a result, he had been apprenticed to an engraver who eventually assigned him to the task of engraving bank notes.

Convinced that he had found the right man, Birch offered Smith a position in the museum as a restorer. As Smith worked in the Assyrian section, he concentrated on cuneiform. By using the keys which others had discovered, he was, in time, able to read the strange markings. While cataloging tablets from Nineveh, he found a tablet which stated that there had been an eclipse of the sun in 763 B.C. Encouraged, he studied the Nineveh tablets more closely.

Intrigued by a rather long passage, Smith set about translating it. Soon the hairs on the back of his neck began to curl, for the story was familiar:

> Tear down thy house, build an ark!
> Give up possessions, seek thou life.
> Despise property and keep thy soul
>   alive!
> Aboard the ship take thou the seed of
>   all living things. . . .

The story-poem went on to tell how the ark was caulked with pitch and how the earth was covered with water. It also asserted that the ark drifted for six days and seven nights. Then after the rains had stopped, the poem stated:

> On Mount Nisir the ark came to a
>   halt.
> Mount Nisir held the ship fast,
> Allowing no motion . . .

14

> When the seventh day arrived,
> I sent forth and set free a dove.

Overwhelmed, Smith requested that Sir Henry Rawlinson check his translation. Rawlinson was impressed. "But there are some missing lines," remarked Sir Henry.

Where were those missing lines?

Smith went through the Nineveh catalogue again and again. But he could not find a single line or even a hint of one. Smelling a sensational story, the *London Daily Telegraph* offered a thousand pounds to anyone who could produce those missing lines. Finally, Smith approached the directors of the museum. "Those lines are in the ruins of Nineveh. Send me. I will find them," he said.

When Smith arrived in Mosul he applied for permission to visit Nineveh. "I'm sorry," said the Pasha. "Permission cannot be granted."

But Smith was stubborn.

Three months after he had sailed, the young, untrained archaeologist was handed a permit. On the 13th day of May Smith noticed a pile of tablets in a ready-to-be-discarded rubbish heap near a Mosul bridge that was under construction. His curiosity aroused, he took the tablets to the hut where he was headquartered. The next morning, after he had dusted them off, he held them to the sunlight and, to his utter amazement, he discovered that he had found the missing tablet! That almost discarded tablet read:

> The dove went forth, but came
>   back;
> There was no resting place for her
>   and she returned.
> Then I sent forth a free swallow.
> The swallow went forth and came
>   back . . .

Eventually, the poem on the slab concluded:

> A raven went forth and, seeing the

> waters diminished,
> He eats, circles, caws and turns not
> around.

(Translated by E. A. Speiser. Princeton University Press, 1950.)

After collecting numerous other items, Smith secured a letter to enable him to take his discoveries through customs. Alas, when he presented his letter at Aleppo, he discovered that he had been tricked. The letter ordered the officials to stop his shipments!

But as stubborn as ever, Smith eventually obtained permission to take his collection to England. The tablet with the missing lines with the poem about the Flood, now resides in the British Museum.

The window lifted by the solution to cuneiform is extremely wide. Among other things, the knowledge that streams through it casts a bright light on the Assyrian Empire which is mentioned 132 times in the Old Testament.

The conquest of cuneiform had been far more productive of useful knowledge than anyone had dared to dream. Nonetheless, this solution solved only part of the problem to the understanding of the past. The next problem was just as formidable as cuneiform. They would have to solve the problem of hieroglyphics! Those birds and strange marks seemed utterly beyond the minds of humankind. But after a groan or two the scholars went to work.

Strangely, even though Egyptian hieroglyphics were seen on obelisks all over Egypt and on the thirteen magnificent ones in Rome, even scholars had merely shrugged at them. This is amazing, for the works of Herodotus were well-known in the New Testament world. Cicero had even dubbed him the "Father of history."

Son of wealthy parents, Herodotus started out on a seventeen-year trip at the age of twenty in 464 B.C. Motivated by curiosity, he noted customs, took measurements, made copious notes, drew maps. Intrigued by hieroglyphic symbols, he wrote: "On the pyramid of Cheops is shown an inscription in Egyptian characters giving how much was spent on radishes, onions and garlic for the workmen. . . ." (*Herodotus*, Book II, H. F. Cary translation).

The work of this skilled writer filled many volumes. But it was largely ignored. Why should anyone bother with Herodotus when they could read Julius Caesar's *Commentaries on the Gallic War*? The first translation of his work into Latin did not appear until 1,875 years after his death!

Ignoring Herodotus, Strabo and others was the fashion. The Western world was not interested in hieroglyphics. And when Christian pilgrims visited Egypt they ignored the strange markings as if they were the works of Satan.

The scene, however, changed. And it was changed in a most unexpected way.

Hoping to conquer Egypt, and thus interrupt Britain's trade with India, Napoleon crowded 35,000 soldiers into 328 ships and landed in Alexandria on July 2, 1798. But his plans were soon crushed, for on August 7 Admiral Lord Horatio Nelson destroyed his fleet near Abukir.

Although trapped, the man who had dreamed of conquering all of Europe, didn't waste time. He had brought along with him a leather-bound edition of Niebuhr's book and one hundred and seventy-five scholars. Book in hand, Napoleon instructed these brilliant men to analyze the treasures in this land of the Pharaohs. His wife, Josephine, had asked him to send her a small obelisk. That was a minor request. He had determined to do much more than that. He would fill France with the cream of Egypt's knowledge!

In later July or early August while the French were enlarging their fortifications near the village of El Rashid (the British call it Rosetta), an Arab workman unearthed a most unusual stone. It was black and crowded with inscriptions. After the basalt slab had been washed, the workers were terrified. They

17

feared it was covered with magical incantations that might summon a plague to destroy them. Fortunately, General Bouchard was summoned before the Arabs could smash it into bits.

Attracted by the three different sets of writing on the slab's surface, Bouchard ordered the stone stored in a safe place. Napoleon was so enchanted he ordered skilled technicians to make exact copies. These were sent to scholars throughout Europe.

The Rosetta Stone, as it came to be called, is eleven inches thick, three feet, nine inches tall, and two feet, four inches wide. It is a trilingual inscription written in hieroglyphics, demotic (a cursive form modified from hieroglyphics), and Greek. Eventually it was deciphered. The Greek translation at the bottom was easy. Reverend Stephen Weston read it in English before the Society of Antiquaries in London in April, 1802.

The hieroglyphic versions obviously had the same meaning as the Greek version. This fact would, of course, make the understanding of the hieroglyphic versions comparatively easy. Not so! Jean Francois Champollion, a French scholar, spent four years at this task, and he was not successful until 1822. With the keys forged by him, we know that the inscription was a decree voted by the "general Council of Egyptian priests assembled at Memphis" to honor the fine things Ptolemy V had done. This Hellenistic ruler of Egypt had lived from 205 to 182 B.C.

Having attained this knowledge, scholars can now read the amazing hieroglyphics produced by the ancient Egyptians. Would you like to read the inscriptions on the largest obelisk in the world? This 455 ton shaft quarried in Aswan out of red granite now stands over 105 feet tall. It was moved from Egypt by an order of Constantine (A.D. 274-337) who intended to have it erected in his new capital—Constantinople. But since he died before this could be accomplished, his son, Constantius, ordered it taken to Rome. It now stands in the Piazza San Giovanni in Laterano. Thus, it is known as the Lateran obelisk.

One of the inscriptions reads:

> He (Thutmose III) made as his monument for his father Amun-Re, Lord of the Thrones of the Two Lands, the setting up for him of a single obelisk in the Upper Court of the Temple in the neighborhood of Karnak, on the very first occasion of setting up a single obelisk in Thebes.

Thutmose III lived from 1504 to 1450 B.C. This means that he and Moses were alive at the same time!

Chapter 2

He Built the Great Pyramid

Now that we can read ancient writing, and have access to scientific methods of approximating dates, the dim millenniums between Creation and the Exodus are coming into focus. Moreover, what we are learning is breathtaking—and Bible-confirming. Carbon-14 tests indicate that farming had developed along the banks of the Nile thousands of years before the birth of Christ.

Those figures mean that human beings were systematically planting seeds thousands of years ago. Indeed, scores of museums have within them the actual bodies of men and women who lived in that distant past.

Would you like to meet Rameses II, believed by some to have been the pharaoh who oppressed the Israelites, and with whom Moses dealt? Such a meeting would be easy to arrange! All one needs to do is to step into the Egyptian Antiquities Museum in Cairo. (Recently he's been in Paris getting treatment for a mysterious rot that has been eating him, but he'll be returning soon.) Confirmed evidence indicates the old man had trouble with his arteries—especially his aorta. Today he would be a candidate for bypass surgery. Also, his knees were seriously calcified.

Rameses II (1304-1238 B.C.), however, was almost sixteen hundred years younger than Khufu—builder of the Great Pyramid. Khufu—the Greeks dubbed him Cheops—ruled

Egypt from 2590 to 2567 B.C. Little is known about him. Still, he is one of the three or four best known pharaohs. Why? Because he built the Great Pyramid at Giza, a short bus ride from Cairo.

The Great Pyramid is the main wonder of the ancient wonders of the world. Its base, alone, covers 13 acres. That is equal to almost ten American football fields. Indeed, it is so wide no archer, standing on its top, could shoot an arrow that would go beyond its base. Altogether, the vast structure contained 2,300,000 blocks of stone. Some of these weigh 15 tons. A mathematician has calculated that if these blocks were cut into one-foot squares and laid end to end, they would reach two-thirds the way around the world.

According to Herodotus, it took ten years to merely build the causeway over which the stones were transported from the Nile; and that it required 100,000 men twenty years to complete the pyramid. Since this pyramid was built merely to become Khufu's tomb, the question is asked: how did Khufu persuade his people to supply the money and to complete this kind of work?

In order to understand that question, we must understand at least an outline of Egyptian history. According to Manetho (c. 305-285 B.C.), an Egyptian priest who wrote the history of Egypt, Egyptian history is divided into 31 dynasties. This seems terribly complicated. But if we condense those dynasties into groups, we get a rough idea about the twists and turns in Egyptian history. Since we must not interrupt the flow of this story, we will list only the main divisions here.

Old Kingdom	2800-2250 B.C.
First Intermediate Period	2250-2000 B.C.
The Middle Kingdom	2000-1786 B.C.
Second Intermediate Period	1786-1575 B.C.
(Hyksos Period)	1700-1570 B.C.
New Kingdom	1575-1085 B.C.
Third Intermediate Period	1085-663 B.C.
Late Period	663-332 B.C.

Khufu, a pharaoh in the Old Kingdom period, had no problem in getting anything he desired— even if it cost the lives of thousands. This power stemmed from the fact that he had royal blood. His father was King Sneferu—founder of the Fourth Dynasty. Moreover, his mother was Queen Hetepheres, daughter and heiress of King Hu (or Huni). Hu had preceeded Sneferu.

This power of lineage, great as it was, was small in comparison to the fact that he was considered divine. The life of Egypt, of course, was the Nile. Its annual flooding every year in July made life possible. No one knew the great river's source. But all knew its value. At the Judgment before Osiris and the Judges of the Dead, each Egyptian was prepared to say: "I have not sullied the water of the Nile, I have not stopped its flow in good times, I have dammed no canal." Because of these values, a pharaoh exclaimed: "May men say of me one day, he was a Nile!"

Khufu was believed to have sufficient power to stop the flow of that nearly 4,000-mile river. He merely had to issue the command! Possessing such power, every word he uttered was immediately obeyed. Believing in immortality, Khufu's great passion was to have his body protected by a tomb where it would perpetually keep its features. This was in order that it would be easily recognized by his *ka* and *ba* when it was time for them to reenter his corpse.

The *ka* was an individual's double. Born with him, it had his characteristics. In a way, it served as a guardian angel. Some were named. Thutmose III referred to his as a "victorious bull who shone in the rings of Thebes." The *ba* was like a soul. It could not leave the body until it died. But it could form itself into any shape it chose and thus had certain magical qualities. The *ka* required food, and because of this requirement, food was placed in the tombs of the dead. The *ba* followed the sun during the night as it visited the underworld. But each morning it hurried back to the body where it lived.

When Khufu considered the fact that he would eventually

die, he immediately began to plan the location of his tomb. It, of course, had to be on the west side of the Nile; for this area of the setting sun was considered to be the habitation of the dead. (When a man died it was stated that he had gone west.) His final decision was brilliant. Khufu had two kingdoms: the Red Kingdom in the north delta region—Lower Egypt; and the vast White Kingdom in the South. By placing his tomb astride the line dividing these kingdoms he would unite them until the end of time!

After selecting the site for what is now the Great Pyramid where he would be entombed, Khufu turned to other priorities. One of these was to remain alive as long as possible.

Khufu felt that he was fortunate in living in Egypt, for this land of the overflowing river was famous for its great physicians. Nearly two thousand years later, Homer (800? B.C.) wrote: "In Egypt the men are more skilled in medicine than any of human kind." This reputation continued. In New Testament times emperors and other wealthy people depended on Egyptian medical men.

In Egypt, Imhotep was considered the father of medicine just as Hippocrates (460?-377 B.C.) is in modern times. Born in approximately 2980 B.C., Imhotep was considered superhuman and made into a demigod. Moreover, many small statues of him were created—and worshiped. Imhotep's fame grew with the centuries, and some twenty-five centuries after his birth he was considered a medical god. All of this was taken seriously; and among those who paid him divine respect was the Roman Emperor, Tiberius Caesar (A.D. 14-37).

What kind of medicine did Imhotep and his followers practice?

Egyptian doctors had names for over 200 parts of the body. They did not understand the circulation of the blood, and they had only one word for veins, arteries, and muscles. Still, they had remarkable skills. Skulls have been recovered from periods even before Khufu which indicate that brain surgery had been practiced. They were also skilled in dentistry. They filled teeth, drained abcesses, did bridgework. They also set bones.

Unusual operations were first tried out on slaves or peasants. If they survived, the same operation might be performed on those of higher rank.

Egyptian doctors depended on three general systems: surgery, medicine, and magic. Some of their prescriptions were rather bizarre. Bloodshot eyes were treated with milk from pregnant women. Those troubled with trichiasis (eyelashes turning inward) were encouraged to pluck their eyebrows, along with their lashes, and to smear their faces with lizard blood.

Mothers with a baby suffering from excessive salivation were instructed to place a live mouse in their baby's mouth, or to have it eat some chopped mice.

Healing magic had many forms. A god-figure was painted on a patient's hand and he was told to lick it off; incantations were written out on papyrus and then allowed to soak in a medicine until the ink was gone, after which the patient drank the medicine. Slumber parties were also arranged in various temples. Then, while the afflicted were asleep, a priest, dressed in the garb of the god for whom the temple was built, would mysteriously appear and give special prescriptions. Such "visions" produced startling results.

Although Cheops had access to the finest medicine and doctors in Egypt, he knew that someday his heart would stop beating. He therefore had long thoughts about his tomb and religion.

In his excellent book, *The Lost Pharaohs*, Leonard Cottrell tells about Egyptian religion: "They believed that in the beginning only the ocean existed, and on this ocean appeared an egg (in some versions a flower) from which was born the sun-god. He had four children, Geb and Shu, Tefnut and Nut.

Planting their feet on Geb, Shu and Tefnut raised their sister Nut to the heavens. Thus Geb became the earth, Shu and Tefnut the atmosphere, and Nut the sky. Geb and Nut had four children, Osiris and Isis, Nepthys and Seth. Osiris succeeded to the throne of his father and governed the world wisely and justly, aided by his sister Isis whom he married. Seth, jealous of his brother's power, plotted to destroy him and eventually succeeded, afterwards cutting the body of Osiris into pieces which he buried in several parts of Egypt. The head was buried at Abydos. The faithful Isis recovered the fragments of her husband's corpse, and with the aid of the jackal-god Anubis, who subsequently became the god of embalmment, re-animated it. Though unable to return to his life on earth, Osiris passed to the Underworld, where he became the god of the dead and later the judge of souls. Isis bore a son, Horus, who afterwards took revenge on his uncle, Seth, defeating the usurper in battle and winning back his father's throne."

How zealous Khufu was for his religious beliefs we do not know. But his reign of twenty-three years was considered an honorable one.

Since the Great Pyramid is the largest tomb ever built for anyone, and since it was built before Egyptians had access to the pulley, wheels, the compass, or explosives, mankind has puzzled how it was done. One thing is obvious. Egyptians in Khufu's time had a thorough understanding of practical mathematics. Otherwise, how did they make the stones fit, form a perfect pyramid, and make its base square with the points of the compass?

Pure mathematics, worked just for the joy of accomplishment, began with the Greeks. Thales (640?-546 B.C.) was so overjoyed when he discovered that any angle inscribed within a semicircle is a right angle that he sacrificed a bull. But *practical* mathematics was being worked by the Egyptians and others thousands of years before the birth of Euclid, Thales, or Pythagoras.

CHEOPS

Visitors to the Far East are amazed at the speed with which a clerk can work out simple mathematics on an abacus. Many can come up with a correct answer quicker than a Westerner with the latest adding machine.

The abacus with its straight wires and beads was in use in Mesopotamia 5,000 years ago!

The startling facts are that these ancients understood elementary astronomy, geometry, a system of writing, used a calendar, and knew how to organize governments.

Even so, they believed in many gods, mummified and worshiped cats, snakes, bulls, and other animals.

Herodotus was so impressed with Khufu's Great Pyramid he wrote at length about it. Today, we know that Herodotus was mistaken in some of his details; but his description is still read, for it provides a *general* idea about how it was done: "A hundred thousand men labored constantly, and were relieved every three months by a fresh lot. It took ten years' oppression to make the causeway for the conveyance of the stones. . . .

"The pyramid was built in steps, battlement-wise . . . After laying the stones for the base, they raised the remaining stones to their places by means of machines formed of short wooden planks . . . There is an inscription in Egyptian characters on the pyramid which records the quantity of radishes, onions, and garlic consumed by the laborers who constructed it; and I perfectly well remember that the interpreter who read the writing to me said that the money expended in this way was 1600 talents of silver. (Each Egyptian talent contained about 56 pounds of silver.) If this is a true record, what a vast sum must have been spent on the iron tools used in the work and in clothing the laborers" (Book II).

Modern engineers believe that Herodotus was mistaken in writing that the stones were raised by machines. Instead, they believe that the stones were pushed up over long ramps made of sand. This idea has now been supported by the discovery of the unfinished pyramid of King Sekhem-khet at Saqqara.

There, the ramps can still be seen.

The immensity of Khufu's accomplishment cannot be comprehended without understanding that although the core masonry came from blocks of limestone cut from nearby quarries, many of the stones were transported by barge up the Nile from quarries hundreds of miles away. In addition, those huge blocks—the average weighed 2-1/2 tons—had to fit!

Eventually, Khufu died. The next problem was to prepare his body in such a way that his *ka* and *ba* would always recognize it. Mummification, even in those early days, was an accomplished art. Herodotus wrote: "The most expensive and best method of embalming is this: First the brain is drawn through the nose with an iron hook, though sometimes solvents are poured into the brain as well. Next, the abdominal cavity is slit open with a sharp Ethiopian stone. The entrails and inner organs are removed and the body is flushed with palm wine and rubbed with ground, pleasantly scented material. The body is then conserved by putting it into hydrated sodium carbonate [natron] longer than seventy days. Then the dead is washed and wrapped in linen bandages. A kind of rubber solution is coated over it, which the Egyptians use instead of glue" (Book II).

All of this having been accomplished the mummy was then placed in a coffin, some of which were made of gold. Each process of mummification was accompanied by elaborate ritual. The final statement was "You live again, you revive always, you have become young again, you are young again, and forever" (*An X-ray Atlas of the Royal Mummies*).

It was because of this belief that pyramids were considered to be houses of eternity rather than tombs.

The jaws of the mummies were kept slightly open so that the *ka* and *ba* could reenter the body at will—and so that the person would be able to plead his cause at the Last Judgment.

Khufu's body went through all these processes, plus many more; nonetheless, even though his mother's remains have been found, his have not. His mummy may have been stolen by grave-robbers.

Unfortunately, the story of mummies does not end in Egypt. James E. Harris and Kent R. Weeks in *X-raying the Pharaohs* have concluded a chapter with a fearful account of the fate of many Egyptian mummies: "Less than four hundred years ago, powdered mummy—ancient human flesh, finely ground—was prescribed by physicians as a treatment for epilepsy, heart murmurs, nausea, poisoning, paralysis, tuberculosis, cuts, bruises—in short, almost every known ailment. Genuine ancient mummies . . . were especially favored by physicians, and by the late 1500s an extensive trade had developed. . . . Some physicians of the sixteenth century, such as Ambroise Pare, criticized the use of mummy, claiming that it caused 'many troublesome symptoms, as paine of the heart or stomake, vomitting, and stinke of the mouth.' But its use has continued. Even today there is a regular, though admittedly not very heavy, demand at a New York pharmacy catering to witches for genuine powdered Egyptian mummy. The cost is forty dollars an ounce."

Chapter 3

The Laws of Hammurabi

In 1895 the French Government made an incredible agreement with Persia. The agreement—purchased with a price—gave the French exclusive rights to make archaeological excavations in Persia, and to retain everything their experts discovered.

By chance, the French began digging at the right place: Susa.

In order to understand why this was the right place, we must think for a moment of the *Fertile Crescent*. The "crescent" section of those words is formed by land arching northward from tips anchored in Egypt on the west and the Persian Gulf on the east. Stretching from the Nile Delta, it bends northward beyond modern Israel, Lebanon, through eastern Turkey, and down Iraq and a portion of Iran to the Persian Gulf. The "fertile" part of those words has two main sources. The banks and nearby land through which the Nile flows are made fertile each year by the annual overflow of that river. In the same manner, Mesopotamia—Greek for *between the rivers*—is enriched by the Tigris and Euphrates which flow on each side.

Surrounded by huge deserts and high mountains, the Fertile Crescent lies between the 30th and 35th parallel—the same lines that cross Arizona, New Mexico, Georgia, and other southern states. This warm climate, plus the fertility of the soil, made it an ideal living area.

These pleasant living conditions gradually persuaded the nomadic hunters to settle down, build houses, and live from the soil. In time, these families began to lay claim to certain plots of land. And living close together meant that the families had to get along with one another and respect boundary lines. Moreover, surplus crops inspired trading with groups who came by their livings in a different way. It was thus that *civilization*—the word comes from the Latin *civis*, which means citizen and implies government—gradually took root.

Susa—Shushan in the Old Testament—was one of the capitals of the Persian Empire and lies some five hundred miles east of the Mediterranean, and just beyond the eastern edge of the Tigris valley. It was here the prophet Daniel was imprisoned by the order of Belshazzar—and it was here that Daniel had his prophetic vision.

Susa had already yielded treasures to the spades of M. Dieulafoy who had labored there between 1884 and 1886. His efforts had uncovered the palace of Artaxerxes Mnemon; and from this palace he had sent to the Louvre in Paris a number of artifacts, including some excellent friezes and many other items.

Inspired by this former success, Jacques de Morgan, a member of Dieulafoy's team, went back to Susa and began digging. Sometime in December 1901 or January 1902 the workers uncovered three sections of a diorite stone which was covered with cuneiform inscriptions. This broken stone when fitted together was 7 feet 4 inches tall, 6 feet 2 inches in circumference at the bottom and 5 feet 4 inches at the top. The cone-shaped mass was covered with many columns of cuneiform script, and at the top there was a bas-relief 26 inches high and 24 inches wide showing a man on a throne handing a rolled script to another man standing before him.

De Morgan was utterly intrigued. Had he discovered something which might prove as important as the Rosetta Stone which was discovered in Egypt a little more than a century before? He didn't know. He would have to wait until the script was deciphered by experts. About two years later, Father Scheil came up with a translation that stunned the world.

The bas-relief showed Hammurabi, king of Babylon, receiving his legal code from Shamash, god of justice. Moreover, the script in the many columns below was that of the code; and, even more intriguing than this was the belief that Abraham had lived at a time when Hammurabi's code was in force.

Would that code explain such problems as the mysterious way in which Hagar was treated? Biblical scholars scratched their heads and went to work. Like the pharaohs and other kings in that period, Hammurabi considered himself divine. The preamble to his code indicates how he felt:

"I, Hammurabi, the perfect king among perfect kings, was neither careless nor inactive in regard to the citizens of Sumer and Akkad, whom En-lil bestowed upon me and whose shepherding Marduk committed unto me. Safe places I continually sought out for them, I overcame serious difficulties, I caused light to shine for them. With the awesome weapons that Zababa and Ishtar entrusted to me, with the wisdom of Ea alloted to me, with the ability Marduk gave me, I uprooted enemies above and below, I extinguished holocausts, I made sweet the expanse of the fatherland with irrigation . . .I am the preeminent king of kings, my words are precious, my ability has no equal. According to the great sun god, the great judge of heaven and earth, may my law be obeyed in the fatherland."

As scholars studied the code and wrote about it, theologians became excited. Could it be that the Amraphel of Genesis 14:1 was Hammurabi? Fascinated, they turned to Genesis 13:18, just before it, and read that together with Genesis 14:1-2. Those passages state:

> Then Abram removed his tent, and came and dwelt in the plain of Mamre, which is in Hebron, and built there an altar unto the Lord. And it came to pass in the days of Amraphel king of Shinar, Arioch king of Ellasar, Chedorlaomer king of Elam,

> and Tidal king of nations; that these made war with
> Bera king of Sodom, and with Birsha king of
> Gomorrah, Shinab king of Admah, and Shemeber
> king of Zeboiim, and the king of Bela, which is
> Zoar.

Thinking that Hammurabi and Amraphel were the same person, they studied a broken bust of Hammurabi which had been discovered. This bust showed a man with a rather long face, curly, terraced beard reaching to his ears, heavy brows, and crowned with a double-tiered, rimless hat. There is a look of authority in his eyes.

While some scholars debated over whether Amraphel was the Hebrew version of Hammurabi, others studied the history of that land between the Tigris and the Euphrates. In Genesis 11:2 they read, "And it came to pass, as they journeyed from the east, that they found a plain in the land of Shinar, and they dwelt there."

Was this Shinar the same as the Shinar in Genesis 14:1? Obviously, yes. But who were they that "journeyed from the east"? The logical conclusion is that they were the close descendants of Noah.

Today, we know about the Sumerians, an ancient people who lived in Sumer. *Harper's Bible Dictionary* refers to Sumer as "the land at the head of the Persian Gulf which became the seat of the oldest civilization in the Fertile Crescent. It occupied the southern part of the rich alluvial plain between the Tigris and the Euphrates, while Accad occupied the northern area of the region. These two countries comprised the later Babylonia. Sumer and its people are important to students of the Bible because their pictographic and semipictographic inscriptions and their Accadian cuneiform documents describe life in the city of Ur in the time of Abraham. . . ."

Sumer did not last. The warm, fertile land, and the easy life became the envy of others. Turmoil, invasion, prosperity, depression, renaissance followed. Then about 2000 B.C. vitality began to return. In time, perhaps three centuries later, Hammurabi—6th king of the First Dynasty of Babylon—came to power. He had an Amorite background.

Hammurabi invaded, conquered, ruled; but for his time, he had a light hand. Desiring unity, he introduced a unique idea by claiming that all of the gods had assembled, and that each had agreed that Marduk, the god of Babylon was the father of all the gods. This being so, he urged all his people to start worshiping Marduk!

Having achieved some unity, Hammurabi built an elaborate capital in Babylon and ruled in splendor. The manner of his rule and life in his day is revealed in the 182 laws of his code, as listed on the columns found in Susa. As we view each law we will do so by the number given it by the translator.

How far had medicine advanced in Babylonia?

> 218. If a doctor has treated a man with a metal knife for a severe wound, and has caused the man to die, or has opened a man's tumor with a metal knife, and destroyed the man's eye; his hands shall be cut off.
> 220. If he has opened his (a slave's) tumor with a metal knife, and destroyed his eye, he shall pay half his price in silver (apparently to the owner of the slave).
> 221. If a doctor has healed a man's broken bone or has restored diseased flesh, the patient shall give the doctor five shekels of silver.

Price fixing is not new. It was done by the Romans—and also by Hammurabi!

> 268. If a man has hired an ox for threshing, twenty qa of corn is its hire.
> 269. If an ass has been hired for threshing, ten qa of corn is its hire.
> 272. If a man has hired a wagon by itself he shall

give forty *qa* of corn a day.

274. If a man hire a son of the people. . . (This scale is not complete, so we will list only the complete ones as listed in the law):

Pay of a potter	five grains of silver,
Pay of a tailor	five grains of silver,
Pay of a carpenter	four grains of silver,
Pay of a ropemaker	four grains of silver. . . .

276. If a man hire a *makhirtu* (a boat), he shall give two and a half grains of silver per diem for her hire.

Wine-sellers, apparently women, were forced to follow strict laws, and the punishment for a violation was severe.

109. If rebels meet in the house of a wine-seller and she does not seize them and take them to the palace, that wine-seller shall be slain.

110. If a priestess who has not remained in the sacred building, shall open a wine-shop, or enter a wine-shop for drink, that woman shall be burned.

Hammurabi's punishments varied with the rank of the offender and the offended. Also, if a son struck his father he was in trouble.

195. If a son has struck his father, his hands shall be cut off.

196. If a man has destroyed the eye of a free man, his own eye shall be destroyed.

198. If he has destroyed the eye of a plebian, or broken the bone of a plebian, he shall pay one mina of silver.

200. If a man has knocked out the teeth of a man of the same rank, his own teeth shall be knocked out.

201. If he has knocked out the teeth of a plebian,

he shall pay one third of a mina of silver.

204. If a plebian strike the body of a plebian, he shall pay ten shekels of silver.

205. If a man's slave strike the body of the son of a free man, his ear shall be cut off.

In that time irrigation had been developed on a large scale as indicated by some laws:

53. If a man has been too lazy to strengthen his dyke, and a breach has opened in the dyke, and the ground has been flooded with water; the man in whose dyke the breach has opened shall reimburse the corn he has destroyed.

56. If a man has opened the waters, and flooded the planted field of his neighbor, he shall measure back ten *gur* of corn for each ten *gan*.

Adultery was severely punished:

129. If the wife of a man is found lying with another male, they shall be bound and thrown into the water; unless the husband lets his wife live, and the king lets his servant live.

Bible students are familiar with the problem Abraham faced when Sarah did not conceive as recorded in Genesis 16. In verse 2 we are told that Sarah suggested that he "go in unto my maid" so "that I may obtain children by her." After Abraham had followed that suggestion, the maid, Hagar, conceived. This caused friction. It seemed to Sarah that Hagar was now looking down upon her. How was the problem solved?

"But Abram said unto Sarai, Behold thy maid is in thy hand; do to her as it pleaseth thee" (vs. 6). Sarah then dealt harshly with her and Hagar fled.

How did this action comply with the laws of Hammurabi? The answer is in section 145 of the code:

> If a man has married a wife and she has not pre-
> sented him with children, and he has set his face to
> marry a concubine; if that man marries a concubine
> and brings her into his house, *then that concubine
> shall not rank with the wife.* (Italics mine.)

Thus, according to the laws of the time, Abraham was perfectly legal in the action he took.

But was Hammurabi really a contemporary of Abraham?
One hundred years ago all of the scholars said yes. Now, many
are inclined to believe that Hammurabi is not really a corruption of Amraphel (Genesis 14:1). When did he live? *The Cambridge Ancient History* suggests 2123-2081 B.C. But these
dates have been revised downward to as low as 1728-1686
B.C. If the newer dates are more accurate and Abraham lived
centuries before Hammurabi, how can we say that Abraham
lived under Hammurabi's Code? The answer is that many of
Hammurabi's laws were merely a codification of much older
laws. Well—the search through history was interesting and
profitable.

The Hammurabi Code was harsh. But a former Babylonian
Code, written in Akkadian (this language went dead about
2000 B.C.), was, in some cases, even more severe. Hammurabi's Code number 142 states: "If a woman hate her husband, and says, 'Thou shalt not possess me,' the reason for her
dislike shall be inquired into. If she is careful, and has no fault,
but her husband takes himself away and neglects her; then the
woman is not to blame. She shall take her dowry and go back
to her father's house."

The older code reads: "If a wife hate her husband and says,
'Thou art not my husband,' into the river they shall throw
her."

Hammurabi's Code number 192 states: "If the son of a *Ner-
sega* (a certain class), or the son of a devotee, to his foster
father or his foster mother has said, 'Thou art not my father,'
or 'Thou art not my mother'; his tongue shall be cut out."

That was cruel indeed. But the older code stated: "If a son says to his father, 'Thou art not my father,' they shall brand him, and fetter him, and sell him as a slave for silver."

Was Moses that cruel? Not quite. At least not quite in every instance! Moses decreed: "Eye for eye, tooth for tooth, hand for hand, foot for foot, burning for burning, wound for wound, stripe for stripe" (Exodus 21:24-25). *But he did not vary the punishment according to the rank of the victim!* "And if he smite out his manservant's tooth, or his maidservant's tooth; he shall let him go free for his tooth's sake" (vs. 27).

According to Hammurabi's Code—201—"If he has knocked out the teeth of a plebian, he shall pay one third of a mina of silver."

(Quotes from Hammurabi's Code and the Older Code are from *The Hammurabic Code* by Chilperic Edwards, Watts & Co., London, 1904.)

Chapter 4

The Unknown Pharaoh

In all literature there are few stories as captivating as the one about Joseph. Sold by his brethren as a slave, he eventually became the grand vizier of Egypt; and, in this position, he was enabled to save the lives of his father and of his brethren who had mistreated him.

The drama is intense. But from a human point of view it is faced with so many problems skeptical people often shrug it off as mere legend.

A main problem of the story is that at this time Egypt had had an unbroken line of pharaohs extending back for thirteen hundred years. These pharaohs had all been rich, powerful, arrogant—and native Egyptians. Moreover, all Egyptians looked with contempt at nomads—and especially those who raised sheep and goats and other small animals. Genesis 46:34 records their current thinking: "Every shepherd is an abomination unto the Egyptians."

Joseph was a slave, a sheepherder—and a foreigner! This being so, how could he become the grand vizier to an Egyptian pharaoh?

The whole idea seems absurd. And yet? Yes, God has a plan; and He works out His plan in ways that are often difficult to understand.

The historian who worked out a list of the pharaohs and their various dynasties, tells us what happened. "We had a king called Tutimaeus. In his reign it happened. I do not know why God was displeased with us. Unexpectedly from the regions of the East, came men of an unknown race. Confident of victory, they marched against our land. By force they took it, easily, without a single battle. Having overpowered our rulers, they burned our cities without compassion, and destroyed the temples of the gods. All the natives were treated with great cruelty, for they slew some and carried off the wives and children of others into slavery. Finally they appointed one of themselves as king. His name was Salitis and he lived in Memphis and made Upper and Lower Egypt pay tribute to him, and set up garrisons in places which would be most useful to him . . . and when he found a city in Sais which suited his purpose (it lay east of the Bubastite branch of the Nile and was called Avaris) he rebuilt it and made it very strong by erecting walls and installing a force of 240,000 men to hold it. Salitis went there every summer partly to collect his corn and pay his men their wages, and partly to train his armed troops and terrify foreigners"(*The Bible as History* by Werner Keller).

These invaders became known as Hyksos which means *rulers of foreign lands.* Coming from Syria and Canaan they conquered Egypt about 1700 B.C. Complete identification and reliable stories about them conflict. Manetho wrote that they sought to "frighten" foreigners. Others wrote that they were "kind" to foreigners.

How did the Hyksos succeed so easily? The Egyptians had grown indolent, overconfident. Also, the Hyksos surprised them, struck suddenly—and with new technology. They used horses and chariots! With horses pounding through their streets, and warriors shooting arrows from bronze chariots, Egypt was overwhelmed.

Now ruled by outsiders, Egyptians ceased to build monuments and scribes neglected to record the day by day events. Egypt was sick and they were sick.

THE UNKNOWN PHAROAH

Undoubtedly it was during this period of the Hyksos that Joseph was brought in chains into the land. Genesis 39:1 tells us this: "And Joseph was brought down to Egypt; and Potiphar, an officer of the guard, an Egyptian, bought him of the hands of the Ishmaelites."

The words, "an Egyptian," in that passage seem rather strange. Why were they used? Perhaps the reason is that almost all of the government officials were foreigners, thus making Potiphar unusual because he was an Egyptian.

As to the Pharaoh, he was undoubtedly a member of the Hyksos. Did they have non-Egyptian pharaohs? A royal mummy or two show that they did!

"Male circumcision, according to Herodotus, was universally practised in Egypt during dynastic times, and evidence of the techniques used has been found in an Old Kingdom relief at Saqqara. It was customary for all males to be circumcised at puberty, yet here was a pharaoh who clearly had not had that operation. . . . Why this was so is not known, but one cannot help wondering if this is not further confirmation of a foreign origin of the late Seventeenth-Dynasty rulers. . . ." (*X-Raying the Pharaohs* by James E. Harris and Kent R. Weeks).

Although this uncircumcised pharaoh was on the throne at the time Joseph was sold to Potiphar, we do not know his name, nor the exact date. But let's go on to the next act in the drama.

Genesis 39:2-5 tells us in crisp, marvelously written words: "And the Lord was with Joseph, and he was a prosperous man; and he was in the house of his master the Egyptian. And his master saw that the Lord was with him, and that the Lord made all that he did to prosper in his hand. And Joseph found grace in his sight, and he served him: and he made him overseer over his house, and all that he had he put into his hand."

Both Joseph and Potiphar continued to prosper. Then trouble began to brew. Potiphar's wife begged Joseph to have an affair with her. (Here we must point out that a story similar to

Joseph's, titled *The Tale of Two Brothers*, was written in hieroglyphics centuries before. Those who write off the Joseph drama as legend claim that this story is merely a repetition of the older one. How foolish! Truth is truth, and all human drama repeats itself again and again.)

Potiphar's wife was persistent. Nonetheless, Joseph continued to resist. Then she caught him in a bad situation. Here's how Genesis 39:11-16 describes it: "And it came to pass about this time, that Joseph went into the house to do his business; and there was none of the men of the house there within. And she caught him by his garment, saying, Lie with me: and he left his garment in her hand, and fled, and got him out. And it came to pass, when she saw that he had left his garment in her hand, and was fled forth, that she called unto the men of her house, and spake unto them saying, See, he hath brought in an Hebrew unto us to mock us; he came in unto me to lie with me, and I cried with a loud voice: and it came to pass, when he heard that I lifted up my voice and cried, that he left his garment with me, and fled, and got him out. And she laid up his garment by her until his lord came home."

The result of this was that Joseph was imprisoned. Having successfully interpreted the dreams of the baker and butler who likewise had been imprisoned, Joseph was eventually summoned to Pharaoh who had also been troubled by a vivid dream.

One can imagine Joseph's fear as he was led through columns of guards armed with spears on the way to the throne. There, the Unknown Pharaoh explained that in his dream he was standing by the river when this action took place.

Genesis records the story: "And, behold, there came up out of the river seven well favored kine and fatfleshed; and they fed in a meadow. And, behold, seven other kine came up after them out of the river, ill favoured and leanfleshed; and stood by the other kine upon the bank of the river. And the ill favored and leanfleshed kine did eat up the seven well favored and fat kine. So Pharaoh awoke" (Genesis 41:2-4).

THE UNKNOWN PHAROAH

Following this dream, Pharaoh had another. The second one was similar to the first, only this one featured ears of corn instead of cattle.

As Joseph, lean from his years in prison, approached Pharaoh, he probably knew that this ruler of Egypt had first consulted with his magicians for an interpretation, and since they had failed, he had followed the butler's suggestion and summoned him.

Joseph's interpretation was that Egypt would have seven bountiful years of harvest followed by seven years of famine. He then had a suggestion: "Now therefore let Pharaoh look out a man discreet and wise, and set him over the land of Egypt. Let Pharaoh do this, and let him appoint officers over the land, and take up the fifth part of the land of Egypt in the seven plenteous years. And let them gather all the food of those good years that come, and lay up corn under the hand of Pharaoh, and let them keep food in the cities" (vss. 33-35).

The Unknown Pharaoh was so pleased with this answer, he made Joseph the second highest officer in all of Egypt. "Thou shalt be over my house, and according unto thy word shall all my people be ruled: only in the throne will I be greater than thou" (vs. 40).

Joseph then arranged for food to be stored all over Egypt, and because of this storage, the lives of his father Jacob and his brothers were saved. Thus, God used an unknown pharaoh to fulfill His purpose.

Are there non-biblical sources that confirm Joseph's stay in Egypt? Yes, there are several. Genesis 41:42-43 explains the ceremony used when Joseph was elevated to his high office: "And Pharaoh took off his ring from his hand, and put it on Joseph's hand, and arrayed him in vestures of fine linen, and put a gold chain about his neck; and he made him to ride in the second chariot which he had; and they cried before him, Bow the knee: and he made him ruler over all the land of

Egypt."

Although there is little evidence of this period from contemporary Egyptian sources, Egyptian murals and reliefs show that this was exactly how such a high official as Joseph would be elevated to power.

But there is other evidence: "The town of Medinet-el-Faiyum, lying eighty miles south of Cairo in the middle of the fertile Faiyum, was extolled as the "Venice of Egypt." In the lush gardens of this huge flourishing oasis grew oranges, mandarins, peaches, olives, pomegranates, and grapes. Faiyum owed these delicious fruits to the artificial canal, over 200 miles long, which conveyed water of the Nile and turned this district, which otherwise would have been desert, into a paradise. The ancient waterway is not only to this day called "Bahr Yusuf"—*Joseph's Canal*—by the fellahin, but is known by this name throughout Egypt. People say that it was the Joseph of the Bible, Pharaoh's "Grand Vizier," as Arab legends would describe him, who planned it" (*The Bible as History*).

Stories and pictographs about a seven-year famine also have been found. In one of the pictographs Egyptians are shown selling corn to a group of people who are clearly Semites. Also, archaeologists have discovered remains of silos where the grain was stored. Their silos, although much smaller than modern ones, were built on similar plans. They even had inside winding steps so that workers could climb to the top and pour in the grain.

Since "Joseph was thirty years old when he stood before Pharaoh king of Egypt" (Genesis 41:46), and since he lived to be one hundred and ten, he undoubtedly served various Pharaohs. These Pharaohs remain unknown.

During the famine, Joseph approached the Pharaoh in power in regard to his family. Pharaoh's answer was prompt: "And Pharaoh said unto Joseph, Say unto thy brethren, This do ye; lade your beasts, and go, get you into the land of

Canaan; and take your father and your households, and come unto me: and I will give you the good of the land of Egypt, and ye shall eat the fat of the land" (Genesis 45:17-18).

When they arrived, Pharaoh assigned Joseph's kinfolk a place to stay—and provided work. Pharaoh said: "The land of Egypt is before thee; in the best of the land make thy father and brethren to dwell; in the land of Goshen let them dwell: and if thou knowest any men of activity among them, then make them rulers over my cattle" (Genesis 47:6).

This land of Goshen on the right bank of the Nile was, and is, an extremely fertile area. The Israelites prospered and then Jacob—Israel—after he had lived in Egypt for seventeen years, passed away at the age of one hundred and forty-seven years (Genesis 47:28).

Jacob was embalmed. Genesis 50:3 informs us that this process took forty days. Here we have a slight problem, for normal mummification took seventy days. The solution may be that the length of time was shorter during the rule of the Hyksos. Also, there are records of various lengths of time used in the procedure.

Joseph, according to his father's wish, took the embalmed body back to Canaan where it still remains. Then, upon Joseph's death, he too was embalmed. However, his mummy did not remain in Egypt. The children of Israel took his bones with them. (See Exodus 13:19 and Hebrews 11:22.)

The Hyksos period continued for a little over one and a half centuries. Then their rulers grew indolent and overconfident. And while they lazed in the sun and asked their butlers for more wine, rebellion began to smoulder in the hearts of the Egyptians. Nonetheless, the Hyksos continued to take life easy. One of their pharaohs even sent a message to a prince in Thebes demanding that he kill all the hippos, for their constant roaring disturbed his sleep!

The pyramids and obelisks reminding them of their glorious past, the Egyptians organized. Then, by using horses and chariots they finally drove the Hyksos out of power and founded a new dynasty, the XVIII, which began about 1570 B.C.

The Hyksos period was over. But the people still remembered. Today museums have within them scarabs (an ancient ornament, often in the form of a beetle, symbolizing immortality) with the name *Jacob-Her* written on them in hieroglyphics. Also, numerous fragments of papyrus relating to the Hyksos period have been discovered. One of them, apparently written by a frontier official says: "I have another matter to bring to the attention of my lord and it is this: We have permitted the transit of Bedouin tribes from Edom via Menephta fort Zeku, to the fen-lands of the city of Per-Atum ... so that they may preserve their own lives and the lives of their flocks on the estate of the king, the good Sun of every land. . . ."

Researchers tell us that the Per-Atum here is the Pithom in the land of Goshen. "Therefore they did set over them taskmasters to afflict them with their burdens. And they built for Pharaoh treasure cities, Pithom and Raamses" (Exodus 1:11).

Some four hundred years after these events a new chapter was reached in the story of the children of Israel. Moses recorded the beginning of that chapter in thirteen words: "Now there arose up a new king over Egypt, which knew not Joseph" (Exodus 1:8).

That fact changed everything!

Chapter 5

Pharaoh of the Oppression and His Daughter

Pinpointing with absolute certainty the pharaoh who ordered male Hebrew children drowned, the princess who rescued Moses from the bulrushes, and the pharaoh of the Exodus, is an impossibility. The best we can do is to weigh the facts on inadequate scales—and guess. There are reasons for this. A major one is that no one has a completely accurate list of these Egyptian rulers. After all, nearly three thousand years is a long time!

There are, of course, several lists. The most celebrated of these is that of High Priest Manetho put together in the third century before Christ. Egyptologists, however, have found errors in it. Then there is the list known as the Abydos List. This one is a list of kings "inscribed upon a wall of the Temple of Abydos by Seti I in the Nineteenth Dynasty" (*History of the Pharaohs* by Arthur Weigall, Vol. 1). In addition, there are several similar lists, each with its good points and weaknesses.

During the Bonaparte era (in the late 1790s), the Turin Papyrus was discovered. This scroll, written in the Seventeenth Dynasty, was located in Egypt, and came into possession of the King of Sardinia. From there, the priceless scroll was shipped in a carelessly packed carton to Turin. When it arrived, the scholars were heartbroken to discover that it had been fragmented into many pieces. In 1826 a group of learned men attempted to reassemble the scroll. The task was all but impossible for many of the fragments were similar to others. How accurate the reassembled scroll is no one knows.

In addition to these lists, there are others such as a fragment of an inscription known as the "Palermo Stone." The puzzle is exceedingly complex. Adding to these problems, there is the problem of chronology. A pharaoh's reign was not figured from the exact day he ascended the throne. Rather it was calculated from one New Year to the next New Year. Thus, if a pharaoh came into power one day before the New Year, that one day was considered an *entire* year in his reign. This means that the entire year, less one day, of the preceding pharaoh was completely discounted in the record of his reign.

Difficult as these complications are, they are just the beginning; for, in addition, they had problems with changing calendars. But in spite of all the puzzles and problems, dedicated scholars have labored long and hard and we have fairly accurate approximations.

The Bible Almanac, edited by James I. Packer, Merrill C. Tenney, and William White, Jr., has an excellent chapter on this subject. They have outlined the arguments for both an *early* and a *later* date of the Exodus. Assuming that the early date is correct, Moses was born in 1526 B.C. If this is so, Thutmose I was the pharaoh who ordered the Hebrew male children drowned. Fortunately, we know quite a bit about him. Indeed, his mummy—No. 61065—is now in the Cairo Museum. Arthur Weigall has described him: "He was a short, broad-shouldered, stocky man, just over 5 feet in height; with a small narrow head, showing a good forehead profile; a delicate, well-shaped nose; the projecting upper teeth characteristic of the family; and somewhat receding, but not weak chin. By the time of his death he had become very wrinkled and completely bald; and there is an expression of shrewdness and cunning about his mouth, which, however, does not detract from a certain general look of refinement" (*History of the Pharaohs*, Vol. 2).

Thutmose I had definite psycholgical problems which must have influenced him in his determination to limit the number of Hebrews in Egypt. But before we look at these, let's go to the first chapter of the Book of Exodus and see what the author of that book had to say about him.

> And the king of Egypt spake to the Hebrew mid-wives . . . and he said, When ye do the office of a midwife to the Hebrew women, and see them upon the stools; if it be a son, then ye shall kill him: but if it be a daughter, then she shall live.
>
> But the midwives feared God, and did not as the king of Egypt commanded them, but saved the men children alive. . . .
>
> Therefore God dealt well with the midwives: and the people multiplied, and waxed very mighty (Exodus 1:8-20).

Terrified about what was happening, Thutmose issued a new order:

> And Pharaoh charged all his people, saying, *Every son that is born ye shall cast into the river*, and every daughter ye shall save alive (Exodus 1:22, italics mine).

It is quite likely that Thutmose's fear stemmed from an inner insecurity. This insecurity may have grown from the fact that he was not the son of the last pharaoh—Amenhotep I who died childless. Rather, he was merely his half-brother. Also, he was undoubtedly the son of Sensonb—a secondary wife. And since inheritance was passed through the female line, he had not received royal blood from his mother. These conditions made his claim to the throne rather shaky. Also, there were other princes who felt that they were entitled to be the new pharaoh.

Thutmose married his half-sister, Princess Ahmhose; but since she, too, was the daughter of a secondary wife, her bloodline was questionable. However, Amenhotep had royal blood from both sides of his family, and since it was understood that he considered Thutmose his heir, Thutmose became the next pharaoh. About this, there is no doubt. Historians even have available to them the proclamation announcing his coronation which took place on "the 21st day of the 3rd month of the 2nd season. . . ." In 1526 B.C. that would have meant around March 12.

By coincidence, the 45- to 47-year-old Thutmose was crowned during the year Moses was born. Indeed, it could be that he started his career by persecuting the Hebrews.

Thutmose expected to be remembered. This can be seen by the royal proclamation which he sent to his governers. He wrote: "Whereas there is conveyed to you this proclamation of the king to notify you that my Majesty has risen as Reed-and Hornet-king upon the Hawk-throne . . . (therefore) make my titulary as follows: the Hawk-king Kenakht-Merimaet (Mighty Bull, beloved of the Goddess of Truth); Lord of the Vulture and Cobra, Khemnesret-Nakhpehti (Ascending in the Cobra-diadem, Great in Strength); Hawk of Nubi, Neferronpitu-Senkhibu (Goodly in years, Refreshing the Hearts); Reed-and Hornet-king, Oekheperkere (Great in the Creation of the Spirit of the Sun-god); Son of the Sun-god, Thutmose (Child of the god Thoth), living for ever and ever. You shall cause sacrifices to be offered to the gods of Iebo (Elephantine) in the South (at a festival which shall be) in the nature of the making of rejoicings in honor of King Oekheperkere who is endowed with (eternal) life. You shall (also) cause the oath to be taken in the name of my Majesty, born of the Royal Mother Sensonb, who is in (good) health. This is a communication to inform you of the matter, and of the fact that the royal House is well and prosperous" (*History of the Pharaohs*, Vol. 2).

PHAROAH OF THE OPPRESSION

Thutmose—there are numerous ways of spelling his name, including Tethmos(is), Thuthmos(is), Touthmos(is), and so on, and biographers say that his title "Mighty Bull" fit him extremely well—is remembered as a successful warrior. During the fall of his coronation year he assembled his battleships, sailed up the Nile, joined his southern army, and faced the Nubians at the Third Cataract.

The Nubians, however, had bitter memories of their defeat by the armies of Amenhotep I and refused to fight. Gloating over his victory, Thutmose had a tablet set up to commemorate the event. The boastful inscription is filled with superlatives.

> He has joined up his frontiers on both sides (of the river), and there is not a man remaining amongst the people of the crimpy hair who would come to attack him. . . The Nubian Bedouin fell by the sword, or were scattered over their territory, so that (the odor of their) putrefying (bodies) flood their valleys, and at the mouths (of their ravines) it was like a violent flood; for their remains were too much for the vultures to pick from them, or carry away. . . Like a young panther amongst a herd in flight, so the fame of his Majesty has dazzled them. He has brought the corners of the earth under his dominion. . . (His fame) has penetrated to regions which his ancestors did not know. . . (*History of the Pharaohs,* Vol. 2).

Thutmose kept expanding his kingdom until his rule extended to the Euphrates. But death caught up with him in about his 58th year. He had ruled 13 years.

At the time of the Pharaoh's death, Moses was entering his adolescence.

Thutmose I had no way of knowing that the Hebrew baby his daughter had rescued would have a far wider fame than his.

To understand these circumstances, we must return to the second chapter of Exodus.

> And there went a man of the house of Levi, and took to wife a daughter of Levi. And the woman conceived, and bare a son: and when she saw him that he was a goodly child, she hid him three months. And when she could not longer hide him, she took for him an ark of bulrushes, and daubed it with slime and with pitch, and put the child therein; and she laid it in the flags by the river's brink. And his sister stood afar off, to wit what would be done to him.
>
> And the daughter of Pharaoh came down to wash herself at the river. . . and when she saw the ark among the flags, she sent her maid to fetch it (Exodus 2:1-5).

Bible readers around the world know the story. Pharaoh's daughter fell in love with the infant in the ark. At that moment, Moses' sister approached. "Shall I go and call thee a nurse of the Hebrew women, that she may nurse the child for thee?" she asked.

When Pharaoh's daughter agreed to this request, Moses' sister summoned his mother, and his mother received wages for caring for her own child. Pharaoh's daughter then adopted him, "and he became her son. And she called his name Moses: and she said, Because I drew him out of the water" (vs. 10).

But who was Pharaoh's daughter? In his *Antiquities of the Jews*, Josephus says flatly: "Thermuthis was the king's daughter." Some modern historians, however, suggest that her name was Hatshepsut and that she was the daughter of Thutmose I. It may be that both names are correct, for royalty often had several names.

A glaring problem about identifying Hatshepsut with

Pharaoh's daughter is that she was allegedly born in 1528 B.C., and this would make her only two years older than Moses! However, a difference of only a dozen years when we are going back around thirty-five hundred years means nothing. Considering that, it is entirely plausible that Hatshepsut, daughter of Thutmose by his half-sister, Ahmose Hent-Temehu, could be the one who rescued Moses and named him.

The early years of Moses in Pharaoh's lavish court are surrounded with mystery—and legend. One incredible story recorded by Louis Golding in *In the Steps of Moses*, is that the rescued baby lifted the crown from Pharaoh's head and placed it on his own. Shocked at what he had seen, the wise man, Balaam, stood and faced the King. "This is no child of Egypt, oh Pharaoh, whom thy daughter has brought into thy house. This is none other than the Hebrew child concerning whom my Master dreamed a dream, and this is the brand which would consume thy house with flame, and the wind which would fan the burning of it . . . Therefore . . . let the counsellors take counsel together. . . ."

The council met and returned with this verdict:

"If it seem good to Pharaoh, let a platter of jewels be set before the child, and a platter of live coals. And if he reach out his hand for the jewels, then it shall be known that he hath done with wisdom all that he hath done, and he shall be slain. But if he stretch out his hand and take the coal, then shall it be known it was without wisdom he did the thing, and he shall live."

This was an unusual test indeed! But Balaam had suggested it after a long consultation with the wise men, and so Pharaoh agreed to the test. As the king of Upper and Lower Egypt, it was important to know if baby Moses had known what he was doing when he took off the Pharaoh's crown and placed it on his own head.

Eyes strained and breath stopped. Pharaoh and his wise

men watched. So much depended on what Moses would do!

"And the child, seeing the platter of jewels and the platter of live coals before him, reached forth to take the jewels, but the angel Gabriel thrust his hand sideward toward the live coals, and he lifted them and burnt his lips and his tongue, and for which reason he was all of his life slow of speech . . . ." (The Jewish Publication Society of America, 1943).

Legend though this is, it indicates the respect the world has for Moses. Moses, however, was a quick learner. Acts 7:22 states: "And Moses was learned in all the wisdom of the Egyptians, and was mighty in words and in deeds."

Where did Moses study? He probably went to Thebes in Upper Egypt or Annu in Lower Egypt, or both. He also had private tutors, as did the children of others in the upper classes.

While Moses was learning, Hatshepsut was busy with her own problems. And she had lots of them. Her main problem was that she passionately wanted to follow her father as the new pharaoh; but she had a half-brother in the way who also longed to be the new pharaoh.

Thutmose I had several wives. But each wife did not have the same quality of royal blood. For example, Hatshepsut's mother Ahmose had richer blood than Mutnofret, the mother of her ambitious half-brother. But in spite of that, her half-brother was coronated as Thutmose II!

Hatshepsut grumbled. She insisted that she had been her father's choice to follow him. However, she did not have enough political support to elbow her half-brother from the throne. And so she did the next best thing. She married him!

Thutmose II was about 5 foot eight inches tall, had protruding teeth like his father, wavy, dark brown hair, broad shoulders, and a receding chin. He kept his finger and toenails carefully trimmed, and was unhappy because early in life he began to lose his hair. He wasn't physically strong. He made up for this lack of strength by assuming such strong titles as Defender of the Sun-god, Son of Amon, and Mighty Bull, Strong and Powerful.

The new Pharaoh had just assumed power when a rebellion broke out in the land of Kush. An inscription tells how Thutmose II dealt with it. "On hearing of this (the rebellion), His Majesty was as furious as a panther. He exclaimed, 'I swear as Re (the Sun-god) loves me, as my father Amon blesses me, I will not let a single one of the men of that family live!' "

But by the time Thutmose II got to Kush, the rebellion had already been crushed and most of the male inhabitants put to death.

As years passed, Hatshepsut's unhappiness increased. She had a daughter by Thutmose whom she proudly named Nofrure—Beauties of the Sun-god. But each day as her maids made up her eyelids and rouged her cheeks, her mind was plotting devious ways to reach the throne.

Then Hatshepsut's world collapsed. A secondary wife of Thutmose had a son who was immediately named Thutmose. This was, indeed, a threat. Ah, but she was expecting. Perhaps her baby would be a son! If so, because of his richer blood, he would outrank the new Thutmose. Alas, her new baby was a girl.

As Hatshepsut waited and plotted, she was constantly annoyed by the lavish attention given to baby Thutmose. He was obviously a favorite. Finally, a desperate Hatshepsut decided that her best course was to be as attractive to her husband as possible in the hope that she would have a son. Then suddenly Thutmose II died. He was only forty. (His mummy is covered with small eruptions. Could it be that he had been poisoned?) The chief architect Ineni left an inscription which reviews those days:

"I possessed the favor of his Majesty every day. I was supplied from the table of the king with bread and beer, meat, lard, vegetables, various fruits, honey, cakes, wine, and oil. . . Then he (Thutmose II) went forth to heaven and was merged into the gods, and his son (Thutmose III) stood in his place as King of the Two Lands."

Hatshepsut, however, became the real power in Egypt.

While intrigue followed intrigue and his adopted mother ruled both Upper and Lower Egypt, Moses had problems of his own. The second chapter of Exodus lifts the curtain for us.

> And it came to pass in those days, when Moses was grown, that he went out unto his brethren, and looked on their burdens: and he spied an Egyptian smiting an Hebrew, one of his brethren. And he looked this way and that way, and when he saw that there was no man, he slew the Egyptian, and hid him in the sand. . . .
>
> Now when Pharaoh heard this thing, he sought to slay Moses. But Moses fled from the face of Pharaoh, and dwelt in the land of Midian. . .(Exodus 2:11-15).

Who was the Pharaoh from whom Moses fled? His adopted mother? Probably not, for she was merely the regent. The *official* Pharaoh was undoubtedly either Thutmose II or Thutmose III.

In Midian, Moses married, raised a family, and became a shepherd. And, undoubtedly, as he stood by the hour watching the sheep, his mind went over the past. And, along with his many memories, bits of information about the current events in Egypt kept coming to him. He was especially interested in what was happening to Hatshepsut, the one who had rescued him from the Nile.

Some of the things Moses learned about the current Egyptian court probably made him shake his head.

About 1485 B.C. Hatshepsut had gained so much power, Thutmose III was almost completely ignored. "I am," she announced, "Daughter of the Sun-god." She also assumed numerous lofty titles, including: *Lady of the Vulture and the*

Cobra and *The Truth of the Spirit of the Sun-god*.
She wrote of herself:

> Her majesty became more important than any-
> one else. What was within her was godlike; godlike
> was everything she did; her spirit was godlike. Her
> majesty became a beautiful maiden, blossoming
> out. The goddess Uto, at this moment, applauded
> her divine shapeliness. She is a woman of dis-
> tinguished appearance. (*Lady of the Two Lands* by
> Leonard Cottrell.)

Today a 1,000 ton obelisk, erected by the order of Hatshepsut, stands in the Karnak temple. Part of the hieroglyphic
inscription on it states:

> And you who after long years shall see these
> monuments, who shall speak of what I have done,
> you will say, "we now know they can have made a
> whole monument of gold as if it were an ordinary
> task" (the obelisks were originally plated with pure
> gold) . . . (*Lady of the Two Lands*).

The lavish inscriptions on this obelisk are merely a sample
of the many similar inscriptions she ordered inscribed on vast
monuments she had built.

Hatshepsut continued to build, boast, and display her
wealth until her death in 1482 B.C. On some monuments she
had herself displayed with a golden beard (the royal insignia),
made flat-chested, and titled: king! Upon her death, Thutmose
III began his active rule.

Instead of killing many of Hatshepsut's servants and bury-
ing them with her as had been done centuries before, small
replicas of her servants were carved and buried with her. After
all, magic would bring them to life when they were
needed. Egypt was making progress!

So far Hatshepsut's mummy has not been conclusively
identified.

Chapter 6

Pharaoh of the Exodus

On the surface it seems amazing that an inscription has not been found in Egypt which names the Pharaoh of the Exodus. But if we ponder a moment we can see why such an inscription was never created. The pharaohs commemorated their successes, not their defeats. The famous memorials to Napoleon's defeats—Waterloo Bridge and Trafalgar Square—are found in London, not Paris!

Who was the Pharaoh that Moses confronted? No one really knows. But scholars have made educated guesses. They suggest that the way to identify that Pharaoh is to know the date of the Exodus. But, being certain about that date is difficult. There are two major schools of thought. One school insists on an early date, while another school pleads for a later date. And so let us first have a look at the arguments for an early date. Those who are inclined this way insist that early Biblical records of time are fairly accurate. On this premise, they go to I Kings 6:1:

> And it came to pass in the four hundred and eightieth year after the children of Israel were come out of the land of Egypt, in the fourth year of Solomon's reign over Israel, in the month Zif, which is the second month, he began to build the house of the Lord.

PHAROAH OF THE EXODUS

Experts believe that Solomon began this work in the spring of 966 B.C. Exodus 12:40,41 gives us another helpful date:

> Now the sojourning of the children of Israel, who dwelt in Egypt, was four hundred and thirty years. And it came to pass at the end of the four hundred and thirty years, even *the self same day* it came to pass, that all the hosts of the Lord went out from the land of Egypt (italics mine).

By adding those dates: 480 plus 966 we come to the figure 1446—and this, they believe, is the date of the Exodus. In addition to this evidence, there is apparent evidence from the Amarna tablets.

The Amarna Letters—so-called because they were discovered in El-Amarna on the east bank of the Nile about 190 miles south of Cairo in 1887—are clay tablets on which diplomatic correspondence was recorded. This correspondence dates as far back as 1413 B.C. This would be a mere 33 years after the beginning of the Exodus and while the Israelites were still on their journey to Canaan.

In this correspondence there are several requests from Canaanite city-states pleading for help to drive out the *Habiru* invaders. But were the Habiru invaders Israelites? By subtracting the 40 years of the Israelites' journeying from 1446— the beginning of the Exodus—we would have the Israelites in Canaan in 1406 B.C. That sounds interesting. Nonetheless, it is not absolute proof that those invaders were the children of Abraham.

Arguments for the later date are set forth in an excellent chapter in Thomas Nelson's *Bible Almanac* which states both positions. "Students who hold this view believe Moses led the Israelites out of bondage during Egypt's nineteenth dynasty, which began in 1318 B.C. The chief line of evidence for the late date is the appearance of new cultural forms in Palestine, specifically the destruction of Jericho by outside invaders at about this date. Scholars who advocate this date point out that the pharaoh of this time was Rameses II (*ca*. 1304-1238 B.C.), and they believe Hebrew slaves built the Egyptian store cities of Pithom and Raamses during his reign (Exodus 1:11; 12:37; Numbers 33:3). Rameses II mentions using slave labor of the *Apiru*—perhaps the Egyptian word for 'Hebrew'—to build his grain cities. Other scholars believe an earlier pharaoh first built these cities, but in that case Rameses II certainly rebuilt and named one of them for himself. Archaeological evidence seems to indicate this. If we assume the Hebrews built these cities for Rameses II, they would have left Egypt some years later, about 1275 B.C., and conquered Canaan after 1235—a date that these scholars believe is confirmed by archaeological evidence that Canaanite cities were destroyed."

Conservative scholars feel that there are far more difficulties encountered if we accept the later date than the earlier one. However, we will look briefly at the Pharaoh who could fit each of these time slots.

Amenhotep II, also known as Amenophis II, (1450—1425 B.C.) was the Pharaoh at the beginning of the Exodus—1446 B.C. If this date is correct and our chronology of the pharaohs is correct, he is the Pharaoh confronted by Moses. What kind of a man was Amenhotep II?

Let's gather the fragments of knowledge about which we can be reasonably certain and study this man from the viewpoint of Moses. Moses went into his self-imposed exile in the land of Midian when he was forty years of age (Acts 7:22-29). He then remained there for another forty years (Acts 7:30). At the end of this time he received his call at the burning bush to lead the children of Israel out of Egypt. He was thus eighty years old when he first presented himself to Amenhotep II.

One can imagine the nervousness Moses felt as he approached the Egyptian capital at Thebes on the Nile over 600 miles south of the Delta. Moses, quite likely, had known Thutmose II and Thutmose I—the grandfather and great-grandfather of Amenhotep II. (Thutmose I was crowned the year Moses was born and Thutmose II was married to his half-sister, Hatshepsut, daughter of Thutmose I, the princess who had rescued Moses as an infant from the Nile and who had raised him. Also, he was probably acquainted with the lad who became Thutmose III and was the father of Amenhotep II.)

Undoubtedly Moses knew the city of Thebes well, for he had probably attended school there. As he entered the magnificent capital, he undoubtedly pieced together all the information he had gathered about Amenhotep II. Much of this information has now been discovered. Thutmose III was a rather small man. But, being a military genius, he is often compared to Napoleon. Altogether, he fought seventeen campaigns. He was buried in the Valley of the Kings; and, like most of the other tombs, his was robbed. But his mummy has been found and can now be seen in the Archaeological Museum in Cairo. His corpse is a tiny brown one, but within his features one can still see the marks of royalty.

In contrast to his father, Amenhotep II was a strong, muscular man. It was said that he could pull a thirty-three-foot oar, and that he was "one who knew horses, without his like in the numerous army, nor was there one in it who could draw his bow" (*Warrior Pharaohs* by Leonard Cottrell).

Indeed, Amenhotep II was very proud of his archery. A stela in Giza declares: "He entered into the northern garden and found set up for him four targets of Asiatic copper of a span (three inches) in their thickness and with twenty cubits (35 ft.) between one pole and its fellow. Then His Majesty appeared in a chariot like Montu in his power. He seized the bow and grasped four arrows at once. He rode northward, shooting at the targets like Montu in his regalia. His arrows came forth from the back of the one target while he attacked the next. And that is a thing indeed which had never been done nor even heard of in story; that an arrow shot at a target of copper came forth from it and dropped to earth, excepting at the hand of a king, rich of glory, whom Amun had strengthened"

(*Warrior Pharaohs*).

Another inscription states: "His Majesty proceeded on his chariot to Khasabu, alone and without a companion, and returned thence in a short time bringing sixteen living Maryannu at the side of his chariot, twenty hands (of slain enemies) at the foreheads of his horses and sixty cattle driven in front of him. . ." (*Warrior Pharaohs*).

Considering how strong and determined Amenhotep was, it is easy to understand why Moses was reluctant to have a confrontation with him.

Amenhotep II died after a reign of twenty-four years. His mummy was entombed in the Valley of the Kings a short distance from those of his father and grandfather. It was discovered in its burial place in 1898. His famous bow was by his side. According to X-ray analysis, he died at approximately forty-five years of age. His was one of the few mummies to be found in the same tomb where it was buried.

From these figures, it would seem that at the time of his confrontation with Amenhotep II, Moses was eighty and the young Pharaoh was only twenty-four or twenty-five.

Assuming that the later date is correct, that the Exodus was during the nineteenth dynasty which began in 1318 B.C., the Pharaoh he confronted was Rameses II—one of Egypt's more famous pharaohs. The highlights of Rameses' career are dramatized on an obelisk which was transported from Tanis and set up near the railway station in Cairo. On the west side of this forty-four-foot shaft are the words:

> The King, the son of Ptah who is
> pleased with victory, who makes great
> mounds of corpses of (Bedouin).

On the south side:

> The one who seizes all lands with
> valor and victory, who establishes the
> Land (of Egypt) again as it was at the
> First Occasion.

The east side:

> A Monthu among kings, who attacks hundreds of thousands, the strong one like Seth when he enters the fray.

The north side:

> The king who smites every land and plunders the land of Nubia (*The Obelisks of Egypt* by Labib Habachi).

Rameses II left many records. These records indicate that he was a man of war. One of them reads: "At evening the captives of every country are brought to the king's tent, and the next morning the plain is seen covered with the dead, especially of the family of the prince of Kheta. The army comes to the king's tent and celebrates his victory in a hymn of praise. . . .Pleased with this flattery, he marches southward, and returns in peace to Thebes, where, of course, he is received with triumphant jubilation by the people" (*Ancient Records of Egypt* Vol. III by James H. Breasted).

According to X-ray studies, Rameses II lived to be 55 plus X years. Some estimates go as high as 85 years. His mummy shows that he suffered from bad teeth and arteriosclerosis. Indeed, his aorta needed immediate bypass surgery.

Chapter 7

Solomon, the Magnificent

In the approximate year, 971 B.C., twenty-year-old Solomon mounted the royal mule, twisted its bridle toward Jerusalem's north gate, and headed toward the Gihon Spring.

It was the day of his coronation.

As Solomon jogged along, he was swept by strong, conflicting emotions. It was great to know that his dying father wanted him to be Israel's third king. On the other hand, it was terrifying to realize that his elder half-brother Adonijah had just proclaimed himself king and that Joab, head of his father's army, had sided with Adonijah. Would there be another civil war like the previous one between another half-brother, Absalom, and his father?

Solomon shuddered. After reigning forty years, his father, David, was on his deathbed. Even the rumor of such a conflict would finish him. Solomon bowed his head and prayed, and as he prayed the recent past returned to him.

In the depths of his heart, Solomon knew that David had planned on making him the new king long before Adonijah had started to openly plot for that position. The fact that his father had arranged for him to marry Naamah, an Ammonite princess, was proof of that. Solomon's great friend at court was the prophet Nathan. Indeed, Nathan respected him so much, he conferred on him another name, Jedidiah, which means beloved of Jehovah.

When word spread that Adonijah was arranging a great public meeting to be centered at the Rogel Well, Nathan immediately arranged for a conference with David. At this conference, he asked the dying king if he had arranged for Adonijah to follow him on the throne. The shock of the question gave David a surge of energy. He signaled for Nathan to leave, and summoned Bathsheba to immediately appear before him. I Kings 1:30 reports that David said to Bathsheba, "Assuredly Solomon thy son shall reign after me, and he shall sit upon my throne in my stead. . . ."

David then summoned "Zadok the priest, Nathan the prophet and Benaiah the son of Jehoiada" (vs. 32), and instructed them that "Zadok the priest and Nathan the prophet [should] anoint him there [at Gihon] king over Israel: and blow ye with the trumpet, and say, God save king Solomon" (vs. 34).

Knowing about these events, Solomon continued on the back of the mule along the route of "heroes" to the Gihon Spring. His coronation is described in I Kings 1:39,40:

> And Zadok the priest took an horn of oil out of the tabernacle, and anointed Solomon. And they blew the trumpet; and all the people said, God save king Solomon. And all the people came up after him, and the people piped with pipes, and rejoiced with great joy, so that the earth rent with the sound of them.

Solomon's coronation produced an immediate, explosive reaction. Rogel Well, where Adonijah's friends were feasting as they celebrated Adonijah's coronation, is only a little over half a mile around a bend in the Kidron from Gihon Spring. When this group heard the trumpets blowing, they were alarmed.

After learning the truth, and discovering that Joab would remain loyal to King David, Adonijah, terrified that he would be executed, fled to the tabernacle and grasped the horns of the altar. (The horns, at the corners of the altar, were used to bind the animals being sacrificed. Traditionally, those seeking safety from the law seized a horn and refused to let go.)

When the report of Adonijah's action reached Solomon, he decreed: "If he will show himself a worthy man, there shall not an hair of him fall to the earth: but if wickedness shall be found in him, he shall die" (vs. 52). This statement led to a reconciliation. But that reconciliation did not last.

Solomon continued to share the throne with David, and then knowing that he was going to die, David summoned Solomon to his bedside for a final word. David's admonition is an oft-repeated one:

> I go the way of all the earth: be thou strong
> therefore, and shew thyself a man; and keep the
> charge of the Lord thy God, to walk in his ways,
> to keep his statutes, and his commandments. . .
> (I Kings 2:2-3).

David then mentioned several problems he felt that Solomon should deal with. One of these concerned Joab who had "murdered" two "captains of the hosts of Israel." The other concerned "the sons of Barzillai the Gileadite." They had sent his army supplies at Mahanaim during the civil war with Absalom; and, as a reward, David desired that they "eat at thy table."

There were also other requests, each of which Solomon fulfilled.

All went well between Solomon and Adonijah, and then Adonijah went to Bathsheba with a strange request. That request was that she approach Solomon and ask permission for him to marry Abishag, David's latest concubine. (This was the Shunammite whom David's servants brought to him in his last days of illness to keep him warm, and with whom he had had no sexual relations. See I Kings 1:1-4.)

The request was an innocent one on the surface. But it had dire implications, for it was customary for the harem of a king to be inherited by his successor. Because of this, Solomon became angry and ordered Adonijah's execution. Later, he also ordered the execution of Joab and others in order to fulfill his dying father's wishes.

Solomon was now on the throne and in complete command of his kingdom which, as the result of his father's conquests, had nearly reached the limits of the territory promised by God to Abraham in Genesis 15:18. "In the same day the Lord made a covenant with Abram, saying Unto thy seed have I given this land, from the river of Egypt unto the great river, the river Euphrates." His kingdom, being larger than it had ever been before or since, Solomon—the name means peaceable—set his heart on a building program, consolidating his territory, and promoting the arts.

Marriage, as it was in Solomon's day, and up to a century or two ago among royalty, had strong political implications. Solomon took advantage of this by marrying the current Pharaoh's daughter. Following David's deathbed-wish, Solomon served the Lord. "And Solomon loved the Lord, walking in the statutes of David his father: *only he sacrificed and burnt incense in high places*" (I Kings 3:3, italics mine).

Solomon sacrificed in the "high places" which later were forbidden because, as yet, there was not a temple equipped for such sacrifices. This is explained in the previous verse: "Only the people sacrificed in high places, because there was no house built unto the name of the Lord."

After sacrificing at Gibeon—a little over five miles northwest of Jerusalem—"the Lord appeared to Solomon . . . by night: and God said, Ask what I shall give thee" (vs. 5). And, as all Bible students know, Solomon replied, "Give . . . thy servant an understanding heart to judge thy people, that I may discern between good and bad. . ." (vs. 9).

God was pleased with this answer, and replied, "Behold, I have done according to thy words: lo, I have given thee a wise and understanding heart; so that there was none like thee before thee, neither after thee shall any arise like unto thee" (vs. 12). Soon the young king's wisdom was put to a test. Two harlots presented themselves to him for a decision. Both had been delivered of a child. Then one of the children died, and Solomon was faced with the duty of deciding to which harlot the live child belonged.

Solomon's decision was unique.

"Bring me a sword," said this son of David.

As the sword was handed to him, the eyes of the women widened. *What is* he going to do? they wondered.

While the women held their breaths, Solomon suggested that the infant be cut in two and divided equally between them. At this point, the true mother, now almost hysterical, cried, "O my lord, give her the living child." But the other one, as cold-hearted as a clam, said, "Let it be neither mine nor thine, but divide it" (vs. 26).

In this fashion, Solomon settled the problem and confirmed to the world that he was indeed a wise man.

Since David had started gathering material for a projected Temple, and since Israel desperately needed a place to worship, Solomon made the construction of this building his first priority. At this time Solomon demonstrated that he had the capacity to organize, and to drive a shrewd bargain. On the whole his subjects were small farmers, not building experts. This meant that he would need outside help in order to build a temple suitable for Jehovah. Looking around, his mind turned toward Hiram, king of Tyre.

Solomon remembered that his father had done business with Hiram before he was born. Indeed, he was the one who had furnished the cedar, masons, and carpenters for the king's palace. In addition, Hiram had demonstrated that he was an excellent builder by enlarging the island city of Tyre, constructing a causeway on the east side in order to connect it to another island, and in planning many beautiful buildings. Having utter confidence in Hiram, Solomon, according to

Josephus, sent him a frank letter.

"Know thou that my father would have built a temple to God, but was hindered by wars, and continual expeditions; for he did not leave off to overthrow his enemies till he made them all subject to tribute. But I give thanks to God for the peace I at present enjoy, and on that account I am at leisure, and design to build a house to God, for God foretold to my father that such a house should be built by me; wherefore I desire thee to send some of thy subjects with mine to Mount Lebanon to cut down timber, for the Sidonians are more skilful than our people in cutting wood. As for wages to the hewers of wood, I will pay whatsoever price thou shalt determine" (*Antiquities of the Jews* by Josephus. Chapter 11, part 6. Josephus probably got his information from I Kings 5:3-9, and II Chronicles 2:3-16).

Hiram agreed to cooperate, and soon his ships, loaded with cargo, were on their way to one of Solomon's ports—probably Jaffa. From this port the material was taken overland to Jerusalem. In compensation, Solomon agreed to annually pay Hiram 220,000 bushels of wheat and 1800 gallons of pure oil. (See *Personalities of the Old Testament* by Fleming James.) In addition, "Solomon gave Hiram twenty cities in the land of Galilee" (I Kings 9:11).

King Hiram, however, didn't like those cities. "And Hiram came out from Tyre to see the cities which Solomon had given him; and they pleased him not . . . And he called them the land of Cabul unto this day" (vss. 12-13).

The conclusion of this story between Hiram and Solomon has puzzled historians—especially since Hiram continued to trade with Solomon and lent him one hundred and twenty talents of gold. (This has been estimated to have weighed 108 lbs.)

But, perhaps, the mystery may have been solved by Frederic Thieberger. He wrote: "If Hiram, as is generally assumed, refused the territory outright, he no doubt demanded compensation; the word *Cabul* expresses contempt on the part of one who smilingly hints that he will not be cheated. But in that case we would expect some mention of another piece of land that Solomon handed over or gave in pledge; moreover, the alliance between the two kings would have suffered such a rupture as to make any further collaboration impossible. Of this, however, there is no evidence. . . . In II Chronicles 8:2, however, a piece of information is preserved that, in view of its detailed form, cannot have been invented at a later time: 'The cities which Huram (the form used throughout the Book of Chronicles) had restored to Solomon, Solomon built them, and caused the children of Israel to live there.' This refers apparently to those same twenty villages on the borders of Phoenicia. *But it would be rash to conclude that Hiram had returned the towns to Solomon immediately*; for what could then the settlement of Israelites mean? Hiram, however, did not have to cede any Phoenician towns; for the debt was Solomon's, not his. The problem is solved as soon as we realize that the verse refers to the *return* of the cities to Solomon after the gold had been repaid. . . . *The produce of the land was, as it were, part of the interest the Phoenicians received*" (*King Solomon*, italics mine).

The third chapter of Second Chronicles outlines the building of the Temple.

> Then Solomon began to build the house of the Lord at Jerusalem in Mount Moriah, where the Lord appeared unto David his father, in the place that David had prepared in the threshing floor of Ornan the Jebusite. And he began to build in the second day of the second month, in the fourth year of his reign (vss. 1-2).

The location of the Temple has been embellished with legends. Moslems declare that the main rock about which the Temple was built has a voice. When Mohammed greeted it: "Hail to thee, O Rock of God!" it answered: "Labbeika, peace be also unto thee, O messenger of God." They also insist that it was from this rock that Mohammed, mounted his horse Burak, took off for heaven; and they point to the footprints of the horse on the rock and claim it is the most sacred spot on the sacred rock.

For Islam, this rock is second only to the Stone of Mecca.

Others claim that Adam built an altar nearby, and that it was here that Cain and Abel parted. Others are certain that it was here that the dreaming Jacob saw the ladder that ascended to heaven; and some even more imaginative groups insist that after Noah's Ark settled, Noah built an altar and sacrificed at this place.

"If we wish to visualize the position of Solomon's Temple with any accuracy," wrote Frederic Thieberger, in *King Solomon*, "the measurements of this rock are our only guide, as no relic of the building itself has survived. The rock, however, has not changed since the time of David, apart from a few steps, indentures and pan-shaped cavities. It lies right across the mountain summit adjacent to the City of David, slightly rising toward the west. At its highest point it stands 80 inches above the ground; its greatest length from north to south is almost 57 feet, its greatest width from east to west over 42 feet."

The Temple itself was not very large. In comparison to Herod's Temple which, with its various courts, occupied nearly 35 acres, Solomon's Temple was merely a chapel. Indeed, it was not built to house worshipers! Rather, it was built for those who went *unto* the House of the Lord, not *into* it.

According to the Westminster Dictionary of the Bible, "The interior of the edifice measured 60 cubits in length, 20 in breadth, and 30 in height . . . The walls were built of stone. . . ." In addition to the actual Temple, there were other buildings— particularly the one dubbed the "Lebanon Forest." This building, erected for assembly and storage was 180 feet long,

90 feet wide, and 54 feet high. It received its name from the four rows of cedars that supported the roof. It was in this building that the two hundred targets and three hundred gold shields were housed. These elaborate showpieces are described in I Kings 10:16-17:

> And king Solomon made two hundred targets of beaten gold: six hundred shekels of gold went to one target. And he made three hundred shields of beaten gold; three pounds of gold went to one shield. . . .

The two hundred targets—smaller shields—similar to the Roman *clipeus*, weighed about five pounds each, while the larger ones, designed to cover most of the body, weighed about twenty pounds.

The gold shields merely indicate Solomon's taste for gold. He was obsessed with gold and used it for every conceivable purpose. He was lavish with gold leaf and with gold inlay. He furnished the Temple with golden candlesticks, golden plates, golden cups. I Kings 10:14 states: "Now the weight of gold that came to Solomon in one year was six hundred and three-score and six talents of gold."

In addition to gold, Solomon loved brass. He employed another Hiram—an architect from Tyre—to build Temple vessels out of bronze. The best known of his creations was the "molten sea." The sides of the elaborate brass container were the thickness of a hand and it had a capacity of 10,000 gallons.

The Temple, using the labor of thousands, took seven years to construct. Small as it was, the fine workmanship, and the huge western retaining wall with its mammoth stones, took time. But Solomon felt the Temple was worth this effort for the Ark of the Covenant needed a permanent home.

This Temple became the symbol of monotheism, and the area on which it rested has undoubtedly been used as a place of worship longer than any other area in the world. Today, the only remnant of Solomon's Temple is the Western Wall, also called the Wailing Wall because of the Jewish custom of praying before it for the restoration of Israel's former power and glory.

Solomon's palace and other buildings required another thirteen years to construct. Vast sums of money were required. Some of this money was earned by Solomon's ventures carried out in the nearby Mediterranean area. The rest came from heavy taxes. In addition, he used forced labor—both his own subjects and members of vassal states.

Possessing almost limitless power, Solomon became a victim of his own vanity. The Bible tells the story. "And all king Solomon's drinking vessels were of gold" (I Kings 10:21). "And all the earth sought to Solomon, to hear his wisdom, which God had put in his heart" (vs. 24). "And the king made silver to be in Jerusalem as stones. . ." (vs. 27).

The sad story is continued in the eleventh chapter of First Kings. "But king Solomon loved many strange women, together with the daughter of Pharaoh, women of the Moabites, Ammonites, Edomites, Zidonians, and Hittites. . . . And he had seven hundred wives, princesses, and three hundred concubines: and his wives turned away his heart. For it came to pass, when Solomon was old, that his wives turned away his heart after other gods: and his heart was not perfect with the Lord his God, as was the heart of David his father. For Solomon went after Ashtoreth, the goddess of the Zidonians, and after Milcom the abomination of the Ammonites. And Solomon did evil in the sight of the Lord. . ." (11:1-6).

Ah, but that wasn't the end. The historians of I Kings continued. "Then did Solomon build an high place for Chemosh, the abomination of Moab, in the hill that is before Jerusalem, and for Molech, the abomination of the children of Ammon. And likewise did he for all his strange wives, which burnt incense and sacrificed unto their gods" (vss. 7-8).

The amount of food needed for Solomon's household was

staggering. Each day he required "thirty measures (335 bushels) of fine flour, and sixty measures (670 bushels) of meal, ten fat oxen, and twenty oxen out of the pastures, and an hundred sheep, beside harts, and roebucks, and fallow deer and fatted fowl" (I Kings 4:22-23).

The Lord chided Solomon for his evil ways. But Solomon would not listen. Finally, the Lord told him what would happen to him and his kingdom.

> I will surely rend the kingdom from thee, and will give it to thy servant. Notwithstanding in thy days I will not do it for David thy father's sake: but I will rend it out of the hand of thy son. Howbeit I will not rend away all the kingdom: but will give one tribe to thy son for David my servant's sake, and for Jerusalem's sake which I have chosen (I Kings 11:11-13).

And so Solomon in all his glory paid a price for his wickedness. Like Saul and David he ruled for forty years. (The length of Saul's reign is not stated in the Old Testament, but Paul and Josephus indicated that it was forty years. See Acts 13:21 and Antiquities VI, 14, 9.) Today he is best remembered for the Temple, his wealth, many wives, and his writings—especially those in Proverbs.

Chapter 8

A Handful of Kings

The Lord had revealed to Solomon that due to his evil ways his kingdom would be divided at the time of his death. Solomon died about 931 B.C. Division followed immediately when his son and successor, Rehoboam, ascended the throne.

This division, although not the nation's first, was tragic.

The Northern Kingdom which split away consisted of ten tribes and was called Israel. It occupied territory slightly smaller than the combined territory of Connecticut and Rhode Island. This meant that the Northern Kingdom had double the population and three times the area of the Southern Kingdom. In addition, the Northern Kingdom was culturally and economically far more advanced. It was also more vulnerable to attack.

During the next two centuries the Northern Kingdom had nineteen kings. In 721, at the end of that time, this kingdom was utterly destroyed by Sargon II, and ceased to exist. (This is the reason those tribes are remembered as the Ten Lost Tribes.) The Southern Kingdom survived until the 590s. Then it was crushed by Nebuchadnezzar and its population exiled to Babylon. Before the exile it had twenty kings. Not having room to sketch each of these thirty-nine kings, we will content ourselves in writing about six—three from ten-tribed Israel, and three from Judah which also included the tribe of Benjamin. The names of all thirty-nine kings—those of Israel plus those of Judah—are listed in the Appendix.

REHOBOAM

At the death of Solomon, Rehoboam was the natural heir to the throne. Rehoboam had royal blood from both sides of the family, for his mother was Naamah, an Ammonite princess— and probably Solomon's first wife.

Unlike Solomon who had inherited a fairly contented kingdom, Rehoboam ascended an extremely shaky throne. His father's overtaxation and labor conscription had angered the entire kingdom—especially the northern section. Rehoboam had an immediate generation-gap problem. As he entered Shechem where he was to be coronated, he asked both the old and the young for advice about what he should say in his coronation speech. After three days of consideration, Rehoboam was ready. Taking advice from the young people with whom he had grown up, he said:

> My father made your yoke heavy, and I will add
> to your yoke: my father also chastised you with
> whips, but I will chastise you with scorpions
> (I Kings 12:14).

The result of Rehoboam's speech was that the northern ten tribes broke away and made Jeroboam their king. Civil war was averted by the concern of Shemaiah who sent the following words to Rehoboam:

> Thus saith the Lord, Ye shall not go up, nor fight
> against your brethren the children of Israel: return
> every man to his house; for this thing is from me
> (I Kings 12:24).

Rehoboam did not go to war with the Northern Kingdom. But he did strengthen his fortresses and war apparatus. Then he allowed Judah to fall into deep sin. The story is told in

I Kings 14:23-24:

> For they also built them high places, and images
> and groves, on every high hill, and under every
> green tree. And there were also sodomites in the
> land: and they did according to all the abomina-
> tions of the nations which the Lord cast out before
> the children of Israel.

In the fifth year of Rehoboam's reign when he was forty-six
years of age, Shishak, the king of Egypt, invaded Judah, and
carried off all the Temple treasures—especially the golden
shields. Rehoboam then replaced the gold shields with
another set made of bronze. Unchecked by this rebuff, he
married Maachah, the daughter of his half-brother Absalom.
Forgetting that the Lord had forbidden him to fight against
the Northern Kingdom, he began to war constantly with them.
After ruling for seventeen years, Rehoboam passed away. He
was forty-eight. He was succeeded to the throne by his
son Abijah.

Altogether Rehoboam had eighteen wives, sixty concubines,
and was the father of twenty-eight sons and sixty daughters.
Second Chronicles tells us that he was "buried in the city of
David" (12:16). But in spite of his wickedness, he was an
ancestor of Jesus! (Matthew 1:7).

JEROBOAM

Jeroboam, the vigorous son of a widow, was a hard worker
and became a favorite with Solomon. Soon the king made him
a foreman over the conscripted laborers who worked on
important building projects. Feeling Solomon's tyranny, he
secretly planned a revolt. These plans were ended by an
unusual twist. First Kings 11 tells the story.

> And it came to pass at that time when Jeroboam
> went out of Jerusalem, that the prophet Ahijah the

Shilonite found him in the way; and he had clad himself with a new garment; and they two were alone in the field: And Ahijah caught the new garment that was on him, and rent it in twelve pieces: And he said to Jeroboam, Take thee ten pieces: for thus saith the Lord God of Israel. Behold, I will rend the kingdom out of the hand of Solomon, and will give ten tribes to thee (vss. 29-31).

Aware of Jeroboam's new attitude, Solomon sought to kill him. Jeroboam saved his life by escaping to Egypt and living under the shadow of their current pharaoh Shishak—the one who looted the Temple. Jeroboam remained there until the death of Solomon. Then, after Rehoboam's coronation, Jeroboam became the king of the Northern Kingdom.

At first, due to the word of the prophet Shemaiah, the rival kings lived at peace with one another. Soon, however, they were at one another's throats. First Kings 14:30 sums up the situation: "And there was war between Rehoboam and Jeroboam all their days."

Jeroboam was in power only a short time when he began to forsake the Lord. Fearful that if his people worshiped at the Temple, they might reunite with Judah, Jeroboam created idols. "Whereupon the king took counsel, and made two calves of gold, and said unto them [his people], it is too much for you to go up to Jerusalem: behold thy gods, O Israel, which brought thee up out of the land of Egypt" (I Kings 12:28). This was merely a beginning of his apostasy.

He employed priests who were not of the tribe of Levi. He promoted fertility cults, adored "all the hosts of heaven," served Baal, and he followed the rites of Molech which "caused their sons and daughters to pass through the fire, and used divination and enchantments" (II Kings 17:17).

Jeroboam's wickedness was so vile, Old Testament historians use the phrase, the "sins of Jeroboam." He ruled for twenty-two years. He was followed to the throne by his son Nadab who was soon murdered by Baasha. Jeroboam's epitaph is a vile one: "He made Israel to sin."

Jeroboam was followed by eighteen kings. Not one of them gave up the golden calves.

HEZEKIAH

Of all the kings of Judah, Hezekiah and Josiah are remembered as the best. The fact that Hezekiah was a great king is a miracle, for he ruled in an era of intense violence, and he was the son of Ahaz—one of Judah's most wicked kings.

Ahaz was an idolator. He sacrificed and burned incense in high places, and he forced his son "to pass through the fire" (II Kings 16:3). When Ahaz was besieged in Jerusalem by Pekah, king of Israel and Rezin, king of Syria, the Lord sent Isaiah to advise him just before the invading armies arrived. Isaiah exhorted him not to call on foreign aid, but instead to rely on Jehovah. Ignoring Isaiah, Ahaz summoned the king of Assyria for aid; and rewarded him out of Temple and palace treasuries. In this tight situation, Isaiah saw a glimmer of hope in the distant future and announced his now well-known prophecy:

> Behold, a virgin shall conceive, and bear a son,
> and shall call his name Immanuel (Isaiah 7:14).

Ahaz, however, was not interested in this prophecy. After Tiglath-pilezer, the Assyrian, had rescued him by lifting the siege, Ahaz went to Damascus and paid homage to him. While there, he saw a heathen altar which he admired. Back in Jerusalem, he had a similar one built and asked his people to bow before it. After a reign of sixteen years, Ahaz turned the throne over to his son Hezekiah. Ahaz, too, was a distant ancestor of Jesus. Only in Matthew 1:9 his name is spelled "Achaz."

Having helped his father rule, Hezekiah was ready for his task. He opened his reign with a series of drastic reforms designed to turn Judah back to Jehovah. He began by cleansing the Temple. Then he removed the idols from the high places. He also arranged a large passover feast and generously invited the ten tribes from the north to share in the celebration (II Chronicles 29:1—30:13). In addition to the images which his subjects had been worshiping was the brass serpent that Moses had created in the wilderness (Numbers 21:9). This piece of brass was so revered, the people were burning incense to it. Disgusted, Hezekiah called it *Nehushtan*—a bronze thing—and ordered it smashed into bits.

As Judah's thirteenth king, Hezekiah was determined to exterminate all idol worship! He revived Temple worship, including animal sacrifices, and the people repented of their idolatry. Second Chronicles 20:20 sums up the results of his efforts: "And the Lord hearkened to Hezekiah, and healed the people." Even so, Judah's troubles were not over.

When Hezekiah received a sarcastic letter from Sennacherib, the Assyrian, telling him that he and his overwhelming hosts would crush Jerusalem, Hezekiah took the letter "up into the house of the Lord, and spread it before the Lord" (II Kings 19:14). He then prayed a realistic prayer: "Of a truth, Lord, the kings of Assyria have destroyed the nations and their lands. And have cast their gods in the fire: for they were no gods, but the work of men's hands, wood and stone: therefore they have destroyed them. Now therefore, O Lord our God, I beseech thee, save thou us out of his hand, that all the kingdoms of the earth may know that thou art the Lord God, even thou only" (vss. 15,17-19).

Isaiah then sent Hezekiah a word of encouragement and assured him the Lord would deliver him. God's deliverance brought about by an angel is outlined in verses 35 through 37. Lord Byron commemorated that famous event when 185,000 Assyrians lost their lives in his brilliant lines:

> For the Angel of Death spread his wings
>   on the blast,
> And breathed in the face of the foe as he
>   passed;

> And the eyes of the sleepers waxed
>   deadly and chill,
> And their hearts but once heaved, and
>   forever grew still!
> (From "The Destruction of Sen-
> nacherib.")

After being delivered from the Assyrians, Hezekiah became ill. Informed by Isaiah that he was about to die, Hezekiah prayed through bitter tears for a few more years of life. There were so many additional things he wanted to do! Moreover, he did not have a son to follow him to the throne. The Lord heard his supplication and granted him an additional fifteen years of life.

Hezekiah ruled for twenty-nine years.

In his genealogy of Jesus, Matthew lists Hezekiah in the tenth verse of the first chapter. There, in the King James Version, his name is spelled Ezekias.

MANASSEH

Manasseh began to rule Judah in 697 B.C. He ruled longer than any other king of Judah. Nonetheless, he was, without doubt, one of the worst kings in history. Strangely, he was the son of Hezekiah, born during Hezekiah's fifteen years extension of life.

Manasseh came to the throne at the age of twelve. And almost immediately he began to undo the good works of his father. Second Chronicles 33 tells both his story and that of his son Amon who followed him.

> But [Manasseh] did that which was evil in the sight of the Lord, like unto the abominations of the heathen ... For he built again the high places which Hezekiah his father had broken down, and he reared up altars for Baalim, and made groves, and worshipped all the host of heaven and served them.

> Also he built altars in the house of the Lord . . . And
> he built altars for all the host of heaven in the two
> courts of the house of the Lord. And he caused
> children to pass through the fire. . .(vss. 1-6).

Manasseh's obvious model was his grandfather Ahaz rather than his father Hezekiah. He took special delight in breaking the Ten Commandments—especially the first two. In addition, he enjoyed condemning innocent people to death. His hands were bloody. Second Kings 21:16 records: "Moreover Manasseh shed innocent blood very much, till he had filled Jerusalem from one end to another."

Among his victims may have been the prophet Isaiah. Rabbinic literature suggests that he had him killed with a saw. One legend has it that the prophet was secured in a hollow tree and that the trunk was then sawn in two. Hebrews 11:37 adds weight to this story. "They were stoned, they were sawn asunder. . . ."

The Lord spoke repeatedly to Manasseh and his people. They refused to listen. So, in punishment, the Lord dealt with them. "Wherefore the Lord brought upon them the captains of the host of the King of Assyria, which took Manasseh among the thorns, and carried him to Babylon" (II Chronicles 33:11).

Penniless and in prison in a foreign land, Manasseh had long thoughts about the past—especially about the way he had ignored the Lord, built heathen altars, and sentenced people to death. And as he thought he must have remembered the way his father had walked with the Lord. In time, he pled for mercy; and the Lord heard him.

Miraculously, Manasseh was allowed to return to Jerusalem; and, even more miraculously, he again occupied his former throne. He then "took away the strange gods, and the idol out of the house of the Lord, and all the altars that he had built in the mount of the house of the Lord, and in Jerusalem, and cast them out of the city" (vs. 15). However, he did not remove the altars from the high places. Nonetheless, his subjects used those altars to make sacrifices unto Jehovah rather than heathen gods.

Manasseh had merely turned *toward* God. He was not *all out* for God!

Altogether, Manasseh ruled Judah for fifty-five years. He was followed to the throne by his son Amon. Amon, it has been suggested, was named after the Egyptian god Amon. With the bias for idols from his father, Amon continued Manasseh's former wickedness. Following two years of rule, he was murdered by his servants. He was succeeded to the throne by his son Josiah who became one of Judah's greatest kings.

Being an ancestor of Jesus, Manasseh is listed in the 10th verse of the first chapter of the first Gospel. In the King James Version his name is spelled Manasses.

AHAB

Shifting to the Northern Kingdom now, Henry H. Halley, in his *Bible Handbook*, lists Ahab as being Israel's worst king, and his father Omri as being "extra bad." Omri, however, although not pious was a credible ruler. He transferred the center of government from Tirzah to Samaria. Indeed, he made such an impression on the Assyrians, cuneiform tablets indicate they called Israel "The House of Omri."

A thumbnail sketch of Omri in I Kings 16, however, reveals his true character: "But Omri wrought evil in the eyes of the Lord, and did worse than all that went before him, for he walked in all the way of Jeroboam. . ." (vss. 25-26).

The story of Ahab brims with melodrama. One of his first mistakes was to marry Jezebel, a princess who was so corrupt few people today would think of naming a child with her name. She was the daughter of Ethbaal, king of Sidon; and, like her father, was devoted to Baal. Moreover, Jezebel so dominated Ahab she persuaded him to at least tolerate Baal worship.

First Kings 22:39 tells us that Ahab built for himself an ivory palace. Since Israel is thousands of miles from the land of elephants, skeptics shrugged at this story. Archaeologists, however, have shown that the Bible is correct. Werner Keller wrote:

"Two great assaults have been made on the old ruined mound of Samaria. The first campaign was led by George A. Reisner, Clarence S. Fisher, and D.G. Lyon, of Harvard University from 1908 to 1910, the second excavation by an Anglo-American team under the British archaeologist J.W. Crowfoot from 1931 to 1935." These two assaults show that "After Omri, Ahab, his son, the new king lived there. He continued building in accordance with his father's plans. The construction was carried out with remarkable skill. . . .

"As the rubble was being carted off, the diggers very quickly noticed the innumerable splinters of ivory that it contained . . . At every step, every square yard, they came across these yellowish-brown chips and flakes, as well as fragments that still showed the marvelous craftsmanship of these elegant reliefs carved by Phoenician masters.

"There was only one explanation of these finds, this palace was the famous 'ivory house' of King Ahab" (*The Bible as History*).

Solomon's foreign wives insisted on having shrines built for their gods. But they did not insist that Solomon and his subjects switch to their faiths. Jezebel was different. She was a Baal worshiper and she insisted that everyone else in her husband's domain also worship Baal. And, in order that she have her way, she imported four hundred and fifty priests of Baal, and had them supported at public expense. Moreover, according to I Kings 18:19, four hundred of them ate at Jezebel's table.

Ahab tried to be neutral in the conflict between Jezebel and the prophets of Jehovah. Indeed, he named his three children with names compounded with Jehovah. His daughter Athaliah's name, for example, means Jehovah is exalted!

This neutrality was too much for Elijah. Finally the time came when he insisted that the people make up their minds.

Having persuaded Ahab to gather his subjects to Mount Car-
mel, Elijah made one of the best known speeches of all
times:

> How long halt ye between two opinions? if the
> Lord be God, follow him: but if Baal, then follow
> him. . . (I Kings 18:21).

In response to this, the writer of that passage commented:
"And the people answered him not a word."

At this point, Elijah asked the priests of Baal to prepare a
sacrifice for their gods and call upon them to set it on fire.
After they had failed, he did the same. In addition, "Elijah
took twelve stones, according to the number of tribes of the
sons of Jacob . . . and built an altar in the name of the Lord"
(vss. 31-32). Next, he had twelve barrels of water poured over
the bullock and the firewood. (Since there was a drought in the
land, the water must have come from the nearby Mediterranean!) The "sons of Jacob" at this time were divided between
Israel and Judah. Hence, Elijah used the symbol of twelve in
order to call attention to the fact that they should be one.

Then, as all Bible students know, Elijah stepped close and
prayed: "Lord God of Abraham, Isaac, and of Israel, let it be
known this day that thou art God in Israel, and that I am thy
servant, and that I have done all these things at thy word. . ."
(vs. 36).

Elijah's prayer was immediately answered. The sacrifice
was consumed, and the people shouted, "The Lord, he is God;
the Lord, he is God" (vs. 39).

Having persuaded the people, Elijah responded with a command: "Take the prophets of Baal; let not one of them escape"
(vs. 40). Elijah then took them to the brook Kishon and put
them to death.

Jezebel glared and never forgot!

The drought having ended, Ahab began to covet Naboth's
vineyard. It was close to his palace in Jezreel and would make
an ideal vegetable garden. Since it had belonged to his father,

Naboth refused to either sell or trade for it, even for a better vineyard. Disappointed, Ahab slumped into deep depression.

To Jezebel, the solution was simple. She had Naboth framed. Her accusation was that he had blasphemed both the king and God! After Naboth had been stoned to death, Jezebel said to her husband, "Arise, take possession of the vineyard" (I Kings 21:15).

Utterly incensed, Elijah responded to this outrage with a shuddering prophecy directed at Jezebel. In spine-tingling words he said: "Thus saith the Lord, in the place where the dogs licked the blood of Naboth shall dogs lick thy blood, even thine" (vs. 19).

Then, speaking directly to Ahab, Elijah added to his prophecy. Said he: "The dogs shall eat Jezebel by the walls of Jezreel" (vs. 23).

Frightened, Ahab tore his clothes, wore sackcloth, fasted, "and went softly." Moved by Ahab's "repentance," Elijah added an addendum to his prophecy. "I will not bring" he quoted the Lord, "the evil in his days: but in his son's days will I bring evil upon his house" (vs. 29).

Several years after these events, Ahab was killed while battling the Syrians. First Kings 22:35 is graphic. "And the battle increased that day: and the king was stayed up in his chariot against the Syrians, and died at even: and the blood ran out of the wound into the midst of the chariot. . . .And one washed the chariot in the pool of Samaria; and the dogs licked up his blood. . ." (I Kings 22:35-38).

Archaeologists not only discovered the remains of Ahab's ivory palace, but also the remains of a large artificial basin nearby. It was probably in this basin that Ahab's chariot was washed and the dogs lapped his blood.

But in spite of the prophecy of the man from Gilead, Jezebel remained alive; and, apparently, happy. Nonetheless, Elijah's prophecy was from the Lord; and therefore would be fulfilled!

Upon Ahab's death, his and Jezebel's son Ahaziah suc-

ceeded him to the throne. Next, while Ahaziah was ruling
Israel, Jezebel's daughter Athaliah married Jehoram, king of
Judah. Thus, one of Jezebel's sons was a king and her
daughter was a queen. Better yet, Athaliah presented Jezebel
with a new grandson, Ahaziah who became the crown-prince of
Judah.

Thinking about her blessings, Jezebel must have laughed at
the words of the poorly dressed, sharp-eyed Elijah.

Ah, but things have a way of changing!

Ahaziah had ruled for only two years when he died as the
result of falling out the palace window. Jezebel was shaken.
But she had another son name Joram. He—the name is also
spelled Jehoram—immediately took his place.

Joram displeased his mother by doing away with the images
to Baal. But he continued to revere the golden calf. Nonetheless, he had a modest belief in Jehovah, and when the king of
Syria sent Naaman to him to be cured of leprosy, Joram
referred him to Elisha. After ruling for a number of years,
Joram was wounded in a conflict with Moab. While he was
washing his wounds at Jezreel, a watchman shouted that Jehu
was approaching.

Alarmed, for Elisha had anointed Jehu king of Israel and
commissioned him to destroy the house of Ahab, Joram
leaped into his chariot, and motioned for his nephew, king
Ahaziah of Judah, to do the same. Second Kings 9 tells
the story:

> And it came to pass, when Joram saw Jehu, that
> he said, Is it peace, Jehu? And he answered. What
> peace, so long as the whoredoms of thy mother
> Jezebel and her witchcrafts are so many. And
> Joram turned his hands, and fled, and said to
> Ahaziah, there is treachery, O Ahaziah. And Jehu
> drew a bow and smote Jehoram between his arms,
> and the arrow went out at his heart, and he sunk
> down in his chariot.
>
> Then said Jehu to Bidkar his captain, Take up,

and cast him in the portion of the field of Naboth the Jezreelite. . . (vss. 22-25).

Ahaziah, grandson of Jezebel, and king of Judah, watched in horror as this terrible drama was being inacted. Then, fearing for his own life, he turned his chariot and fled. But he was not quick enough.

And Jehu followed after him, and said, Smite him also in the chariot. And they did so at the going up to Gur, which is by Ibleam. And he fled to Megiddo, and died there (vs. 27).

In this fashion, Jezebel lost her son Joram, king of Israel, and her grandson, king of Judah. What was her response? The history of her last hours is related in II Kings 9:30-37.

And when Jehu was come to Jezreel, Jezebel heard of it; and she painted her face, and tired [adorned] her head, and looked out at a window. And as Jehu entered in at the gate, she said, Had Zimri peace, who slew his master? And he lifted up his face to the window, and said, Who is on my side? who? And there looked out to him two or three eunuchs. And he said, Throw her down. So, they threw her down: and some of her blood was sprinkled on the wall, and on the horses: and he trode her under foot.

And when he was come in, he did eat and drink, and said, Go, see now this cursed woman, and bury her: for she is a king's daughter. And they went to bury her: but they found no more of her than the skull, and the feet, and the palms of her hands.

Wherefore they came again and told him. And he said, This is the word of the Lord, which he spake by his servant Elijah the Tishbite, saying, In the portion of Jezreel shall dogs eat the flesh of Jezebel: And the carcase of Jezebel shall be as

dung upon the face of the field in the portion of Jezreel; so that they shall not say, This is Jezebel.

Was that the end of the house of Ahab? Not quite! Jezebel's
daughter Athaliah, queen of Judah, seized the throne after
Jehu murdered her son, Ahaziah. Next, she murdered all of
her grandchildren with the single exception of Joash who was
rescued and hidden by his aunt Jehoshabeath.

Few careers have had the violent ups and downs as the career of Athaliah. She was the queen of a king for eight years.
Then she was a queen mother for twelve months. And finally,
she became the ruling queen for six years. But her glitter did
not last. After her grandson Joash was installed as the king of
Judah, she was murdered at the place where "the horses came
into the king's house" (II Kings 11:16).

Joash didn't last long. His servants killed him while he was
in bed.

HOSHEA

Hoshea, son of king Elah who was murdered by Zimri, and
who murdered his predecessor, king Pekah, has the distinction
of being Israel's last king. His rule was ended by the Assyrian,
Sargon II.

Hoshea—the name means save or salvation and was
Joshua's original name (Deuteronomy 32:44)—ruled from 732
B.C. to 723 B.C.

Sargon II ended Hoshea's rule by crushing Israel. Actually,
Hoshea reaped what he had sown, for he had conspired with
the Assyrian king Tiglath-pileser to get rid of Pekah by mur-
dering him.

Although not the worst of kings, Hoshea was not zealous for
the Lord. Israel remained full of heathen groves and high
places. When Israel was invaded by Shalmaneser V, king of
Assyria, Hoshea kept him at bay by paying tribute. Soon,
however, the Assyrians were in trouble with Egypt. Sensing an
advantage, Hoshea refused to make his tribute payment. This

was too much for Shalmaneser. Second Kings 17:4 relates what happened: "And the king of Assyria found conspiracy in Hoshea: for he had sent messengers to So king of Egypt, and brought no present to the king of Assyria, as he had done year by year: therefore the king of Assyria shut him up, and bound him in prison."

Shalmaneser laid seige to Samaria; but, in spite of his superior forces, Samaria held out for three years. Then, following the death of Shalmaneser, Sargon II, Assyria's new king, took over. Cuneiform texts tell us what happened. Sargon II boasted: "In the first year of my reign, I besieged and conquered Samaria. . . .I led away into captivity 27,290 people who lived there."

Where did Sargon II take those captives? Second Kings 17:6 reports that he "placed them in Halah and in Habor by the river of Gozan, and in the cities of the Medes." Since these captives were "chief citizens" Israel was no more.

The area where Sargon exiled his prisoners cannot be identified. But some researchers believe it was in Mesopotamia, north of Haran. Perhaps the river Gozan was a tributary of the Euphrates.

But Sargon was not satisfied to merely move his captives into his own country. No, indeed! He had additional plans. The writer of II Kings reports:

> And the King of Assyria brought men from Babylon, and from Cuthah, and from Ava, and from Hamath, and from Sepharvaim, and placed them in the cities of Samaria instead of the children of Israel: and they possessed Samaria, and dwelt in the cities thereof (17:24).

The mixed blood that followed this exchange of population is one reason Samaritans in New Testament times were held in such contempt.

Israel's final year was 723 B.C. This date is certain because Sargon II declared that he captured Israel the year he came to power. Historians have cuneiform proof that Sargon mounted the throne just after Shalmaneser's death which occurred unexpectedly in 722 in the midst of the conquest of an important Palestinian city.

Sargon apparently accepted the reins of government while still out in the field.

Chapter 9

God's Servant: Nebuchadnezzar

Nebuchadnezzar—also spelled Nebuchadrezzar—son of Nabopolassar, was one of the greatest and most contradictory kings who ever warmed a throne. The pendulum of his character swung from one extreme to another. After a battle, he frequently pointed to a prisoner and said, "Skin him alive!" Or, if he was in a different mood, he ordered his prisoners to eat at his own table—and to gorge.

Moreover, Nebuchadnezzar's moods changed by the hour.

But in spite of this, the distinguished prophet Jeremiah, inspired by "the Lord of hosts" wrote that "Nebuchadrezzar the king of Babylon" was a "servant" of the Lord (Jeremiah 25:9).

Nebuchadnezzar strode into history in a characteristically flamboyant way. After a two-month siege Nineveh had fallen to a military alliance made up of Medes, Babylonians, and Scythians. The date was August, 612 B.C. Flushed with triumph, Nabopolassar ordered his son Nebuchadnezzar to keep going until he had conquered Egypt.

Nabopolassar knew that his son could be trusted. Starting at the bottom as a day-laborer in Babylon, Nebuchadnezzar had worked himself to the top. He was efficient, confident, talented, hardworking. A black cameo in the Berlin Museum shows him wearing a heavy brass helmet. The helmet covers his ears and surrounds his throat. His triangular nose, firm chin, determined eyes, and unsmiling lips, indicate a man who knew what he wanted and was willing to pay the price.

As Nebuchadnezzar and his troops continued toward Egypt they broke down city walls, fired buildings, killed prisoners. All were confident that the land creased by the great river would soon be theirs. On, on they continued. Soon Memphis was in the distance. With a little effort the famous city would be theirs. His men licked their lips. Then an unexpected trumpet blew.

The chariot with the foaming horse stopped at Nebuchadnezzar's tent. The anxious courier from Babylon had startling news. King Nabopolassar was dead!

Without a moment's thought, Nebuchadnezzar made up his mind. "I must go to Babylon," he said.

"What about Memphis?" asked a commander.

"We'll take care of Memphis later!"

Riding hard, Nebuchadnezzar pressed on toward Babylon; and within three weeks he was sitting on the throne with a crown on his head. He was then the most powerful man on earth—and he knew it!

When one of Nebuchadnezzar's wives, a princess from Media, complained about the flatness of Babylon, he was ready with a plan. "Never mind," he said. "I will make you a series of gardens that will be finer than any you've ever seen. We'll have flowers, palms, fruit. When I've completed them they'll be one of the wonders of the world!"

"But there's no rain in Babylon," argued his wife.

"Rain? We don't need rain." He pointed to the Euphrates flowing through the western side of the city. "We'll build pumps. Babylon is destined to be the most beautiful city built by men. Babylon's god Marduk is guiding me!"

The so-called Hanging Gardens of Babylon didn't really hang. Instead, like a many-layered cake they consisted of terraces built on top of one another. The 200-square-foot terrace on the summit was 350 feet above the lowest one. These terraces were covered with thousands of tons of rich soil. Water was pumped to a tank on the top and it flowed downward. There were even fountains. Also, there was a sprinkling system to produce artificial rain.

Soon the terraces were covered with foliage, palms, exotic flowers. Travelers from many lands made trips to Babylon just to see the gardens.

Nebuchadnezzar smiled at their interest. But his mind kept going back to Nineveh. He still remembered how the men looted the city, using their axes to cut away slabs of gold, and to hack out precious jewels from incredible statues. Moreover, he had heard of Solomon's Temple in Jerusalem. Soon he was counting the days when he could leave Babylon for more conquests. In his mind's eye he could see trains of mules carting the spoils back to Babylon.

In Jerusalem, the prophet Jeremiah, sick of Judah's evil ways, was prophesying that the city would be destroyed. Again and again he approached the rulers, insisted that they repent, and reminded them that the city was doomed. Said he: "Thus saith the Lord; Behold, I set before you the way of life, and the way of death. He that abideth in this city shall die by the sword, and by the famine, and by the pestilence. . .For I have set my face against this city for evil, and not for good, saith the Lord: it shall be given into the hand of the king of Babylon, and he shall burn it with fire" (Jeremiah 21:8-10).

But Jeremiah's message was not all gloom. In the distant future he saw the dim light of the coming Messiah: "Behold, the days come, saith the Lord, that I will raise unto David a righteous Branch, and a King shall reign and prosper, and shall execute judgment and justice in the earth" (Jeremiah 23:5).

Likewise, he had good news for the near future. That good news was that their punishment would have an end: "And this whole land shall be a desolation, and an astonishment; and these nations shall serve the king of Babylon seventy years. And it shall come to pass, when seventy years are accomplished, that I will punish the king of Babylon. . ." (25:11-12).

In 606 B.C. Nebuchadnezzar swooped down on Jerusalem. This was during the third year of the reign of Jehoiakim. He besieged the city "And the Lord gave Jehoiakim king of Judah into his hand, with part of the vessels of the house of God" (Daniel 1:2).

Since he had defeated Judah, why did he not crush it and add it to his empire? Tribute! With his building projects he needed money, and Judah was ready to supply him with money.

Nebuchadnezzar was impressed with Jerusalem and with the skill of the people. Because of this, he took back with him the finest minds in the nation just as we did at the end of World War II. Daniel relates what happened: "And the king spake unto Ashpenaz the master of his eunuchs, that he should bring certain of the children of Israel, and of the king's seed, and of the princes; children in whom was no blemish, but well favored, and skilful in all wisdom, and cunning in knowledge, and understanding science, and such as had ability in them to stand in the king's palace, and whom they might teach the learning and the tongue of the Chaldeans.

"And the king appointed them a daily provision of the king's meat, and of the wine which he drank: so nourishing them three years, that at the end thereof they might stand before the king.

"Now among these were of the children of Judah, Daniel, Hananiah, Mishael, and Azariah. . ." (Daniel 1:3-6).

The new king rubbed his hands with joy. It was unbelievable what he, Nebuchadnezzar, had accomplished! In the depths of his being he realized his own greatness. His torture chambers made the world fear him, and the drawings on his walls of his devious torture methods impressed foreign dignitaries about the fate of those who disagreed with him. In addition to his organizational and building genius he was broadminded. Did he fear the brilliant minds of other nations? Lesser kings did. Not he! He licked his lips and clapped for more wine. As proof of his broadmindedness, he thought of his brilliant Hebrew prisoner Daniel, renamed Belteshazzar, and of Belteshazzar's fellow prisoners: Hananiah, Mishael, and Azariah, now honored with the exciting names: Shadrach, Meshach, and Abednego.

Again and once again Nebuchadnezzar clapped for additional wine.

As he sipped the wine, glanced at the lewd pictures on the wall, let his feet sink into the expensive carpet, his mind went back to Daniel. Yes, that young Hebrew had related the dream he, His Majesty the King, had not revealed. And he had even had the courage to tell him that he, the head of gold, would be replaced. What a man! He had ordered others skinned alive for exhibiting much less courage. Ah, but how had he, King Nebuchadnezzar, King of Kings responded? He had made Daniel the chief governor over all the wise men and ruler of the entire province of Babylon! And as for Shadrach, Meshach, and Abednego? Yes, he had given them high positions in the government.

A little wobbly from wine and self-satisfaction, Nebuchadnezzar staggered off to bed.

In the morning he had a new idea. Daniel tells us about it.

> Nebuchadnezzar the king made an image of gold, whose height was three-score cubits, and the breadth thereof six cubits: he set it up in the plain of Dura, in the province of Babylon (3:1).

Next, a herald announced: "O people, nations, and languages . . . at what time ye hear the sound of the cornet, flute, harp, sackbut, psaltery, dulcimer, and all kinds of musick, ye [shall] fall down and worship the golden image that Nebuchadnezzar the king hath set up: and whosoever falleth not down and worshippeth shall the same hour be cast into the midst of a burning fiery furnace" (3:4-6).

Bible readers remember that Shadrach, Meshach, and Abednego refused to bow to the image. This meant that they were sentenced to the "fiery furnace." Tossing criminals into a blazing furnace was a common practice in those days and for centuries later. Volume IV of *Voyage en Perse* by Chardin, published in 1735, has a paragraph on this subject: "The practice of throwing certain criminals into a furnace survived in Persia. . . . Ali Kulikhan . . . caused a great kiln to be built on the Royal Square and another on the Public Square, and ordered the criers to publish that those who should sell bread at a higher price than that allowed, or concealed grain, would be thrown in alive. These ovens burned continually for a month, but no one was thrown in, because no one would run the risk of such a drastic punishment by disobedience" (*Nebuchadnezzar* by G. R. Tabouis.)

The Prophet Daniel recorded what happened to the three Hebrew youths in the third chapter of his book. "These men were bound in their coats, their hosen, and their hats, and their other garments, and were cast into the midst of the burning fiery furnace . . . because the king's commandment was urgent, and the furnace exceeding hot, the flame of the fire slew those men that took up Shadrach, Meshach, and Abednego.

"And these three men, Shadrach, Meshach, and Abednego, fell down bound into the midst of the burning fiery furnace. Then Nebuchadnezzar the king was [astonished], and rose up in haste, and said unto his counsellors, Did not we cast three men bound into the midst of the fire? They answered and said unto the king, True, O King. He answered and said, Lo, I see four men loose, walking in the midst of the fire, and they have no hurt, and the form of the fourth is like the Son of God" (Daniel 3:21-25).

After the Hebrew youths were removed from the furnace, Nebuchadnezzar examined them closely, and he discovered that not a single one of their hairs had been singed, nor had "the smell of the fire [been] passed on them." Overwhelmed, Nebuchadnezzar exclaimed: "Blessed be the God of Shadrach, Meshach, and Abednego, who hath sent his angel, and delivered his servants. . ." (vs. 28). Then Nebuchadnezzar lifted his voice. In verse 29 Daniel recorded what he said: "Therefore I make a decree, That every people, nation, and language, which speak any thing amiss against the God of Shadrach, Meshach, and Abednego, shall be cut in pieces, and their houses shall be made a dunghill: because there is no other God that can deliver after this sort."

While Nebuchadnezzar was beautifying Babylon, invading other nations, and making decrees, Jehoiakim continued to rule in Jerusalem—and send tribute to Babylon. Unfortunately, this son of Josiah was not popular with his subjects. After a rule of eleven years, he either died or was murdered. Of him, Jeremiah wrote: "They shall not lament for him, saying, Ah my brother! or, Ah sister! they shall not lament for him, saying, Ah lord! or, Ah his glory! He shall be buried with the burial of an ass, drawn and cast forth beyond the gates of Jerusalem" (22:18-19).

Upon Jehoiakim's death, his son, Jehoiachin, mounted the throne. This young man—according to II Kings 24:8 he was a lad of only eighteen—ruled for a mere three months and ten days when Nebuchadnezzar's generals returned to Jerusalem in 597 B.C. This time the Babylonians carried away "all the treasures of the house of the Lord, and the treasures of the king's house" (II Kings 24:13). Also they "cut in pieces all the vessels of gold which Solomon king of Israel had made in the temple of the Lord. . ." (vs. 13).

In addition, they took Jehoiachin, his wives, servants, mother, and princes. Altogether, they made ten thousand captives and marched them back to Babylon. "None remained, save the poorest sort of the people of the land" (vs. 14).

Nebuchadnezzar then changed the name of Mattaniah, one of Josiah's sons, to Zedekiah, and appointed him a puppet king over Judah. All went well until Zedekiah refused to pay additional tribute. This was the end. Nebuchadnezzar returned in 586. This time it took him a year and a half to complete his conquest. He knocked down the walls, burned the Temple, destroyed the city. Zedekiah and some top officials fled. But they were captured near Jericho. Nebuchadnezzar then ordered Zedekiah's sons put to death as their father watched. Next, Zedekiah was forced to kneel while his eyes were put out. According to wall reliefs, this was done with a spear.

Jerusalem was no more.

The conquest had taken twenty years. The date was 586.

The destruction of Jerusalem was heartbreaking. Nonetheless, Daniel continued to serve Nebuchadnezzar. Then the king had another dream—this one about a tree that reached to heaven. Frantic to know the answer, Nebuchadnezzar summoned Daniel. The meaning of the dream was so fearful, Daniel hated to interpret it. But, being true to his convictions, he faced the king. This is what he said: "This is the interpretation, O king, and this is the decree of the most High, which is come upon my lord the king:

"That they shall drive thee from men, and thy dwelling shall be with the beasts of the field, and they shall make thee to eat grass as oxen, and they shall wet thee with the dew of heaven, and seven times shall pass over thee, till thou know that the most High ruleth in the kingdom of men, and giveth it to whomsoever he will" (Daniel 4:24-25).

All of these things came to pass, just as Daniel had prophesied.

Many who do not accept the Bible as being *the* Word of God have doubts about Nebuchadnezzar's madness. Concerning the king's period of insanity, George Rawlinson in *The Five Great Monarchies*, wrote: "Toward the close of his [Nebuchadnezzar's] reign, when his conquests and probably most of his great works were completed, in the midst of complete tranquility and prosperity, a sudden warning was sent him ... This malady has been termed 'Lycanthropy' ... the great king became a wretched maniac ... His subjects generally, it is probable, were not allowed to know of his condition, though they could not but be aware that he was suffering from some terrible malady." And, in a note, Rawlinson added: "He was no doubt strictly confined to the private gardens attached to the palace."

Daniel has given us a vivid description of Nebuchadnezzar during the period of his insanity. "He was driven from men, and did eat grass as oxen, and his body was wet with the dew of heaven, till his hairs were grown like eagles' feathers, and his nails like birds' claws" (Daniel 4:33).

In time, Nebuchadnezzar regained his sanity. He died in 562 and was succeeded by his son Evil-Merodach who kindly released Jehoichin from prison and gave him a permanent place at his table.

Evil-Merodach was accused of lawlessness and put to death in 560.

Chapter 10

His Knees Thumped

The Jewish exiles in Babylon were mostly from the upper classes, and they lived well. Babylon was a prosperous city; and, as always, the Jews knew how to adapt to the new situation. Moreover, they had good connections. Daniel and the three men who survived the fiery furnace had high positions.

Within a few years the Jews had learned the arts of their new environment: law, medicine, banking. Also, they learned the magic of compound interest! Nonetheless, they had long thoughts about Jerusalem—even though Jerusalem had been destroyed. An immortal psalm comes from this era:

> By the rivers of Babylon, there we sat down, yea, we wept when we remembered Zion.
>
> We hanged our harps upon the willows in the midst thereof. For there they that had carried us away captive required of us a song; and they that wasted us required of us mirth, saying, Sing us one of the songs of Zion.
>
> How shall we sing the Lord's song in a strange land? If I forget thee, O Jerusalem, let my right hand forget her cunning (Psalm 137:1-5).

As the years ground by, one can imagine the exiles reliving the past. "My father knew Jeremiah well," related a storekeeper, "and his eyes used to glow when he remembered that Jeremiah prophesied that we would serve the king of Babylon seventy years. 'Seventy years,' he used to say, 'just seventy years. Seventy years is a long time. But seventy years, son, is only threescore and ten!' "

"Yes, and he mentioned seventy years more than once," replied a dim-eyed old man whose straggly beard was like snow on his chest. "Listen, I'll quote his exact words: 'For thus saith the Lord, That after seventy years be accomplished at Babylon I will visit you, and perform my good word toward you, in causing you to return to this place' " (Jeremiah 29:10).

But how were those seventy years to be measured? Would they be measured from Nebuchadnezzar's first invasion, or his second invasion, or his third invasion when he destroyed the Temple and burned the city?

At this point Belshazzar enters the picture.

But who was Belshazzar? Some critics have been disturbed because history indicates that Belshazzar was not the son of Nebuchadnezzar as is stated by Daniel in his book, chapter five verse two. That, however, is no problem; for frequently in the Old Testament the word father simply means a paternal relative. There are many examples of this. Genesis 28:13 refers to Abraham as being the *father* of Jacob when actually he was his *grandfather*. The same procedure is followed in II Samuel 9:7 where Mephibosheth is stated as being the *son* of Saul when in reality he was a *grandson*. (Speaking of a distant paternal individual as being the father was also used in secular writings in this period.)

The fifth chapter of Daniel opens with the words, "Belshazzar the king." This has been questioned, for historians once believed that Nabonidas was the last king of Babylon. However, contemporary cuneiform evidence plainly states that Nabonidas empowered Belshazzar with kingship during his third year. No, there is no contradiction. Belshazzar was co-regent with special jurisdiction over the city of Babylon.

Still, we have not been shown how Nebuchadnezzar could have been either the father or even distant relative of Belshazzar. Raymond Philip Daugherty in his fascinating book *Nabonidas and Belshazzar* may have put the puzzle together. "The queen who steps on the stage in Daniel 5:10 is conversant with the things that occurred in the court of Nebuchadnezzar, *for her solicitude appears to be that of a mother*. It has been shown that the consort of Nabonidas was the queen whom Herodotus calls Nitocris" (italics mine). The writer then shows that Nitocris was probably the daughter of Nebuchadnezzar. Assuming this is correct, Nebuchadnezzar was the grandfather of Belshazzar!

Before us is one of the greatest dramas known to mankind, a drama that completely altered history; and, in a most unusual and dramatic way.

Daniel 5:1 opens the curtain. "Belshazzar the king made a great feast to a thousand of his lords, and drank wine before the thousand."

That there should be a feast at this time seems incredible, for Babylon was being besieged. Cyrus and his army were just outside the walls. Indeed, the Persians had already occupied some of the suburbs! Nonetheless, Belshazzar was confident. Herodotus has left us a few lines which explain his source of confidence.

"A battle was fought a short distance from the city, in which the Babylonians were defeated by the Persian king, whereupon they withdrew within their defences. Here they shut themselves up, and made light of his siege, *having laid in a store of provisions for many years in preparation against this attack*; for when they saw Cyrus conquering nation after nation, they were convinced that he would never stop, and that their turn would come at last" (Herodotus, Book 1; italics mine).

In addition to the provisions, Belshazzar had complete faith in the city's walls. After all, Nebuchadnezzar had made them indestructible. At least that is what he thought when he wrote: "In order to strengthen the defences of Esagila that the evil and the wicked might not oppress Babylon, that which no king had done before me, at the outskirts of Babylon to the east I put up a great wall. Its moat I dug and its inner moat-wall with mortar and brick I raised mountain-high. About the sides of Babylon great banks of earth I heaped up. Great floods of destroying waters like great waves of the sea I made to flow about it; with marsh I surrounded it" (*Building Inscriptions of the Neo-Babylonian Empire* 1, by S. Langdon, Paris, 1905. Quoted from *Babylon* by Joan Oates).

The outer wall which surrounded the eastern and southern parts of the city consisted of three parallel walls. The innermost wall was nearly 23 feet thick. The next wall, 39 feet farther out, was a little thicker and was built of baked brick. Then, beyond this, was another baked-brick wall nearly ten feet thick. Next, the walls were surrounded by a moat which, in places, was over three hundred feet wide.

But that wasn't all. The spaces between the walls were filled with vast quantities of rubble. In addition, there were heavy fortifications.

Inside the outside walls, there were two more parallel walls: the *Imgur-Enhil* and the outer *Nimitti-Enlil*. The Imgur-Enhil was over 21 feet thick, while the Nimitti-Enlil was 13 feet thick.

Fully one-third of the city of Babylon consisted of fortifications. The west side of the city was protected by the Euphrates. Since there was a sewer that some determined enemy might enter, Nebuchadnezzar had his engineers fix it in such a way it could not be entered. He wrote: "In order that no pillaging robber might enter into this water sewer, with bright iron bars I closed the entrance to the river, in gratings of iron I set it and fastened it with hinges. The defences of Esagila and Babylon I strengthened and secured for my reign an enduring name."

Feeling secure in the center of all these fortifications,

Belshazzar made a daring move. Daniel tells us about it: "Belshazzar, whiles he tasted the wine, commanded to bring the golden and silver vessels which his father Nebuchadnezzar had taken out of the temple which was in Jerusalem; that the king, and his princes, his wives, and his concubines, might drink therein. Then they brought the golden vessels that were taken out of the temple of the house of God which was at Jerusalem; and the king, and his princes, his wives and his concubines, drank in them" (5:2-3).

The banquet hall where this drinking—Herodotus tells there was also dancing—took place was a very large one. Archaeologists, having examined the ruins, estimate it was 195 feet by 178 feet in size. This means that if there were one thousand guests, each one had available to him about 35 square feet.

How was the hall decorated? The Borderasiatisches Museum in Berlin has rebuilt a decorated facade of the throne room which was separated from the banqueting hall by a large doorway. The rebuilt wall in Berlin is approximately forty feet high. It is made of glazed brick with a colorful intricate design of columns and flowers. The bricks forming the lions at the base are cleverly placed to give a third-dimensional look to the animals, which are made of several colors: yellow, white, blue and red.

It was a sumptuous place!

As the lords were drinking and the golden and silver vessels from the Temple in Jerusalem were being refilled, Nitocris, daughter of Nebuchadnezzar, and mother of Belshazzar, must have thought about some of her recent projects. One of these has been described by Herodotus. This project was one which would "leave another monument to her reign over Babylon."

"She [Nitocris] gave orders for the hewing of immense blocks of stone, and when they were ready and the basin was excavated, she turned the entire stream of the Euphrates into the cutting, and thus for a time, while the basin was filling, the

104

natural channel of the river was left dry. Forthwith she set to work, and in the first place lined the banks of the stream within the city with quays of burnt brick, and also bricked the landing-places opposite the river-gates. . ." (Herodotus, Book 1).

Turning her mind back to the feast, Nitocris participated in the wild drinking, singing, and laughter. Raised in the palace of Nebuchadnezzar, she had learned to revel in feasts, orgies, drinking-bouts. Daniel tells us what happened.

> They drank wine, and praised the gods of gold, and of silver, of brass, of iron, of wood, and of stone. In the same hour came forth fingers of a man's hand, and wrote over against the candlestick upon the plaster of the wall of the king's palace: and the king saw the part of the hand that wrote (5:4).

As Belshazzar stared at the hand, the entire group stared; and during the painful silence the only sounds that could be heard were made by those who had already had too much to drink. Then another sound, a soft thumping sound, broke the intense quiet. Daniel reported:

> Then the king's countenance was changed, and his thoughts troubled him, so that the joints of his loins were loosed, and his knees smote one against another (vs. 6).

Suddenly the king began to speak. His eyes were wide and his voice shook. Here's what Daniel wrote:

> The king cried aloud to bring in the astrologers, the Chaldeans, and the soothsayers. And the king spake, and said to the wise men of Babylon, Whosoever shall read this writing, and show me the interpretation thereof, shall be clothed with scarlet, and have a chain of gold about his neck, and shall be the third ruler in the kingdom (vs. 7).

BELSHAZZAR

The lords in the banqueting hall were almost breathless as they watched the wise men study and try to interpret the words of the mysterious hand. They knew the Arabic words read, "Numbered, numbered, weighed, divided," but what did the message mean? While the wise men studied, pulled their beards, and gaped, an unusual activity was going on outside. Herodotus wrote about that activity. "He [Cyrus] placed a portion of his army at the point where the river enters the city, and another body at the back of the place where it issues forth, with orders to march into the town by the bed of the stream, as soon as the water became shallow enough: he then himself drew with the warlike portion of his host, and made for the place where Nitocris dug the basin for the river, where he did exactly what she had done formerly: he turned the Euphrates by a canal into the basin, which was then a marsh, on which the river sank to such an extent that the natural bed of the stream became fordable. . ." (Herodotus, Book 1).

Unable to interpret the handwriting, the experts finally gave up. Nitocris then approached the throne and suggested that the king summon Daniel. Since it was then 539 B.C. and Daniel had been taken in his youth to Babylon by Nebuchadnezzar in 606 B.C., he must have been an old man in his late eighties. But answering the summons, for he was always obedient, he stood before the king.

The king made him the same offer of gifts which he had made to the others. These, Daniel refused. But, bent though he was, and as frightening as the interpretation was, Daniel faced Belshazzar. This is what he said:

> And this is the writing that was written, Mene, Mene, Tekel, Upharsin. This is the interpretation of the thing: Mene; God hath numbered thy kingdom, and finished it. Tekel; Thou art weighed in the balances, and art found wanting. Peres; Thy kingdom is divided, and given to the Medes and

Persians (Daniel 5:25-28).

After Daniel had finished, an order was given; and he was clothed in scarlet and a gold chain was placed around his neck. But even in the midst of the ceremony, the Persian army was entering the city. The last two verses of the fifth chapter of Daniel, using a mere twenty-five words, explain what happened:

> In that night was Belshazzar the king of the Chaldeans slain. And Darius the Median took the kingdom, being about threescore and two years old.

Cyrus, himself, tells us what followed. "As I entered Babylon in peace, and established my royal residence in the palaces of the princes amidst the jubilation and rejoicing, Marduk, the great lord, warmed the hearts of the Babylonians toward me, while I for my part devoted myself daily to do him reverence. . .The dwellers in Babylon. . .I freed from the yoke that ill became them. I repaired their houses, I healed their afflictions. I am Cyrus, king of all, the great king, the mighty king, king of Babylon, king of Sumer and Akkad, king of the four corners of the earth. . . ."

When the exiled Jews in Babylon awakened to the fact that the city had been conquered by the Persians, they must have remembered that Jeremiah had prophesied: "And it shall come to pass, when seventy years are accomplished, that I will punish the king of Babylon. . ." (Jeremiah 25:12).

Had seventy years passed? The first deportation from Jerusalem had taken place in 606 B.C. It was now 539 B.C.— 67 years later! Was the Lord ahead of schedule? Possibly. But possibly the punishment of the Babylonians was still in progress!

Chapter 11

God's Shepherd: Cyrus

He was born under a sentence of death, founded a great empire, executed his enemies, signed a decree that changed the course of civilization—and was killed by a woman. Even so, the Prophet Isaiah stated flatly that this man was God's shepherd (Isaiah 44:28—45:1). Moreover, Isaiah's statement proved to be correct even though he made it two centuries before the subject of his prophecy mounted the throne. In addition, Isaiah named the man!

I refer to Cyrus the Great.

Herodotus wrote more primary history about Cyrus than anyone else. From his pen we have an intriguing story about the birth of this king. "Astyages . . . had a daughter who was named Mandane, concerning whom he had a wonderful dream. He dreamt that from her such a stream of water flowed forth as to not only fill his capital, but to flood the whole of Asia. This vision he laid before such of the Magi as had the gift of interpreting dreams, who expounded its meaning to him in full, whereat he was greatly terrified. On this account, when his daughter was now of ripe age, he would not give her in marriage to any of the Medes who were of suitable rank, lest the dream should be accomplished; but he married her to a Persian of good family. . .Thus Cambyses [the Persian] took her to his home. . . ."

Then Astyages had another dream. This one made him wring his hands and pace the floor; for, according to the interpretation, his daughter would have a son who would replace him and rule over all of Asia! Utterly desperate, he ordered Mandane to return home. When he learned that she was pregnant, he became hysterical.

After summoning a faithful servant by the name of Harpagus, he gave an order. "Take the child of Mandane: carry him with thee to thy home and slay him there. . . ."

Harpagus promised to obey the order. But when the time came to kill the child he didn't have the courage. Instead, he turned him over to a herdsman. "Astyages," he said, "requires thee to take this child and lay him in the wildest part of the hills, where he will be sure to die speedily. And he bade me tell thee, that if thou dost not kill the boy, but allowest him to escape, he will put thee to the most painful of deaths. . . ."

The herdsman took the boy home. There, he learned his wife had just been delivered of a stillborn child. Immediately she fell in love with Mandane's son; and so she adopted him, and gave her own son a royal funeral in order to deceive Harpagus.

This story of Herodotus is probably a myth, and the story about how young Cyrus discovered that he had royal blood is even more fantastic. Nonetheless, these are some of the tales that surround the birth and childhood of Cyrus.

Eventually the genius of Cyrus was recognized. He ascended his royal grandfather's throne and banished his grandfather into exile. Next he amalgamated Media and Persia. When he was attacked by Croesus of Lydia, the man famed for his riches, he defeated him and seized his capital. He was then prepared to attack Babylon.

Babylon fell to Cyrus as we noted in the last chapter. Being of a liberal mind, he decided to allow the Jews and numerous other exiles to return to their homelands. The decree he signed is recorded in the first chapter of Ezra:

109

> The Lord God of heaven hath given me all the kingdoms of the earth; and he hath charged me to build him an house at Jerusalem, which is in Judah. Who is there among you of all his people? his God be with him, and let him go up to Jerusalem, which is in Judah, and build the house of the Lord God of Israel, (he is the God,) which is in Jerusalem. And whosoever remaineth in any place where he sojourneth, let the men of his place help him with silver, and with gold, and with goods, and with beasts, beside the freewill offering for the house of God that is in Jerusalem (1:2-4; the "court record" of this decree is in Ezra 6:3-12).

In addition to this, "Cyrus the king brought forth the vessels of the house of the Lord, which Nebuchadnezzar had brought forth out of Jerusalem, and had put them in the house of his gods; even those did Cyrus king of Persia bring forth by the hand of Mithredath the treasurer, and numbered them unto Sheshbazzar, the prince of Judah" (1:7-8).

As the ecstatic Jews read and heard those almost unbelievable words, they were reminded of the prophecies of Jeremiah—and of Isaiah who had referred to Cyrus as God's shepherd—Isaiah 44:28—and who had written, "Thus saith the Lord to his anointed, to Cyrus. . ." (45:1).

This edict was signed 538 B.C.

Although God had used him to do His will, just as He used Nebuchadnezzar and Alexander the Great to do His will, Cyrus the Great never became a follower of God. He still clung to the gods of Babylon, especially Marduk. Indeed, one of his first projects when he conquered Babylon was to restore the images and shrines to their various deities.

The story of the death of Cyrus is wrapped in almost as many legends as the story of his birth and rise to power. Again, for the best answer we must go to Herodotus. He wrote: "At this time the Massagetae (they were on his northeastern frontier in central Asia) were ruled by a queen named Tomyris, who at the death of her husband, the late king, had mounted the throne. To her Cyrus sent ambassadors, with instructions to court her on his part, pretending that he wished to take her to wife. Tomyris, however, aware that it was her kingdom, and not herself that he courted, forbade the men to approach. Cyrus, therefore, finding that he did not advance his designs by this deceit, marched toward the Araxes, openly displaying his hostile intentions, set to work to construct a bridge on which his army might cross the river, and began building towers on the boats which were to be used in the passage.

"While the Persian leader was occupied in these labors, Tomyris sent a herald to him, who said, "King of the Medes, cease to press this enterprise . . . Be content to rule in peace thy own kingdom . . . As, however, I know thou wilt not choose to hearken to this counsel . . . leave . . . bridge-making. Let us retire three days' march from the river bank, and do thou come across with thy soldiers; or, if thou likest to give us battle on thy side of the stream, retire thyself an equal distance."

Cyrus decided to face her army on her side of the stream.

Herodotus continued: "First, the two armies stood apart and shot their arrows at each other; then, when their quivers were empty, they closed in and fought hand-to-hand with lances and daggers" (Herodotus, Book 1).

Eventually, Cyrus was killed and his army defeated. His rule of twenty-nine years had been brought to an end by the army of a woman.

Cyrus was buried in a modest tomb built of white limestone near the Persian royal residence of Pasargadae. The empty tomb still stands. It is close to Shiraz in southeastern Iran.

Did he realize that by sending the Jews back to Jerusalem he had changed the course of history? Probably not. Still, he had been used by the Lord!

Chapter 12

Alexander the Great

Understanding the ancient world during the four centuries before Christ appears to be more difficult than it really is. Confronted by such baffling terms as Seleucids, Ptolemies, and Hellenization, many readers share the frustrations of a Stone Age savage when first confronted with print. This is unfortunate, for without the knowledge of those centuries, we miss a dimension in our understanding of both the Old and New Testaments. This need not be, for a casual understanding of those convulsive centuries is quite easy if one has the proper key.

The proper key is Alexander the Great.

Most of us know that Alexander all but conquered the world by the time he was thirty-two. But few realize that he also arranged the world's largest marriage ceremony—there were nine thousand couples!—and provided a trade language for the world that helped spread Christianity.

King Philip of Macedon had an excellent cavalry made up of the finest horsemen of Macedonia. And he took pride in knowing that his finest officers could ride anything equipped with hooves. But in 342 B.C. his pride was bent by a huge black horse—Bucephalis. This snorting, bucking, concentration of twisting fury was more like a bolt of lightning than a horse. No officer could mount him.

"Let me try," begged Philip's fourteen-year-old son Alexander.

"It's impossible!" replied the one-eyed king.

Alexander would not give up. "Please. I know I can ride him."

After some hesitation Philip agreed. Then he became stern. "You may try. But you may try only once. If you fail—" He paused to let the words sink in. "If you fail you'll have to buy the horse. The price is thirteen talents!" (That was equivalent to 80,000 drachmae. Skilled workers in Athens earned two drachmae a day.)

Alexander knew that if he failed it would require a lifetime to repay the debt. But he didn't believe in failure. Pushing by the strong-muscled men who'd been tossed into the dust, he grasped the bridle in a firm hand and turned Bucephalis until he faced the sun. Then he addressed him in low, reassuring tones. Soon the hysterical horse began to calm.

The moment the majestic head was lowered, Alexander leaped on his back. Next, still forcing the head into the sun, Alexander eased his new friend into a gentle canter. After he had ridden him a while, he galloped over to his father.

"How did you do it?" asked the astonished king.

Alexander replied that he had noticed that Bucephalis was afraid of his own shadow and that he had eliminated that terror by forcing him into the sun so that his shadow was behind him. Overwhelmed, Philip kissed the blue-eyed youth on the head. Then with great emotion, he made a solid declaration. "Macedonia will not be big enough for you!"

Few have started life under the kind of tensions and actions young Alexander faced. Born in 356 B.C., he was almost literally cradled in thunder. His father, King Philip, was the son of King Amyntas II, and had assumed the throne when he was only twenty-three. Philip was an enlightened man. Nonetheless, his gnawing ambition was to conquer the world. War was his favorite occupation and young Alexander became accustomed to seeing him dressed in armor.

But as violent as Philip was, he was no match for Olympias—his wife. Moreover, Olympias was cunning. She believed in witches, omens, oracles. Also, she was willing to do anything—even commit murder—in order to have her own way.

Olympias' romance with Philip started on the Island of Samothrace. (Paul stopped there four hundred years later on his way to Macedonia.) She was the daughter of the former king of Epirus. Thus Alexander had royal blood from each side of the family.

From the beginning of their marriage Olympias was a problem. For one thing she adored snakes. Indeed, she kept them in the bedroom! When Philip objected, she claimed that they were not only tame but holy. And so in love was she with her snakes she allowed them to crawl over her body and even encircle her neck.

The day of Alexander's birth, Philip was away fighting and had to be informed by special messenger. That day turned out to be a special one. In addition to the news about his son, the king learned that one of his horses had taken first prize in the Olympics and that his troops had won an important victory in Illyria.

Three bits of good news in one day was an excellent omen!

Highly pleased, Philip decided that Alexander was to become much greater than himself; and so he hired Aristotle to be his tutor. This famous teacher imparted to the lad a fierce hunger for knowledge. Among other things, he introduced him to Homer's *Iliad*. The book utterly captivated Alexander. He memorized most of it and always kept a copy under his pillow. His special copy had notes in it by Aristotle. The mythical Achilles, hero of the *Iliad*, became Alexander's model. And this devotion became even more intense when his mother insisted that he was related to Achilles.

Early, Alexander learned that he was a crown prince and

behaved accordingly. When asked, "Will you compete in the Olympic foot-races?" he replied, "I won't run against anyone except kings!"

Philip left Alexander in charge at the capital city of Pella while he went south to Greece. Taking advantage of Philip's absence, a northern tribe revolted. This was a made-to-order opportunity for Alexander. Without bothering for permission, he headed north and crushed the uprising. Then he renamed the city Alexandropolis in his own honor.

Soon Philip tired of snakes. He replaced Olympias with Cleopatria, a young Macedonian. Crimson with rage, Olympias planned revenge. She began by turning Alexander against his father.

At a feast of celebration, one of Cleopatria's uncles got drunk. In this condition, he expressed the wish that Philip and Cleopatria would have a son. He then suggested that this son would be a pure Macedonian and thus the ideal successor to the throne.

"What about me?" demanded Alexander. "Am I not the lawful heir?"

In a drunken stupor, Philip whipped out his sword and went after Alexander. But he was so wobbly he crashed to the floor. Facing the group and in sneering contempt, Alexander cried, "Look, Macedonians! This man says he's going to lead you from country to country in Asia. But he can't even walk from one table to the next!"

Still, Alexander admired his father. The old man had had an eye shot out by an enemy arrow; limped because of a wound; and had a nearly useless arm as the result of another war injury. Yet he fought with the tenacity and skill of a youth. On one occasion when Philip came limping home, his good eye alight with victory, Alexander burst into tears. Why? Because he feared his father would conquer so much territory there would be none left for him to conquer!

Philip was assassinated during Alexander's twentieth year. The deed climaxed a plot that may have included Olympias.

ALEXANDER

Alexander was ready. He rounded up the suspects, executed them, and mounted the throne.

At this time revolt rumbled throughout Greece. Alexander, however, deceived the rebels. Instead of marching south, he turned north and kept going until he reached the Danube. There, he pitched his tents where modern Bucharest stands. Having crushed the tribes causing the trouble, he returned to Macedonia. From here he pounced on Greece.

The city of Thebes, in central Greece, had been unusually insolent. After they spurned his terms, he burned their city and sold thirty thousand inhabitants into slavery. But he spared one home—that of Pindar, a man whose poetry he admired.

Now that Greece and the northern tribes were settled, Alexander turned the administration of his kingdom over to his general, Antipater, and prepared to invade Persia—modern Iran. At that time, Persia covered nearly half the world. Moreover, King of Kings Darius III, was able to raise an army of one million. He also had a formidable navy.

Such a mighty army seemed overwhelming to everyone but Alexander. His confidence in himself and in his generals was absolute. His staff included such reliables as Ptolemy, Seleucus, Parmenion, and Cleitus.

Before setting out in 334 B.C., Alexander consulted the oracle at Delphi. The priestess refused to say anything. She declared that it was a poor time to prophesy. Angered, Alexander forced her into the temple and compelled her to prophesy. "Young man," she replied, "you will be invincible!"

Scoffing at the size of the Persian army, Alexander launched his invasion with less than 30,000 foot soldiers and only 4,000 cavalrymen. This means he was outnumbered nearly thirty to one. Moreover, the Persians were on homeland while he had supply problems.

Approximately four centuries later, the Apostle Paul

invaded Europe from Asia by the way of Macedonia; now Alexander was invading Asia by the way of Macedonia. Alexander's army crossed the Hellespont in 334. As for himself, the young conqueror followed the footsteps of his hero—Agamemnon. Steering a vessel with his own hands, the blue-eyed warrior landed at Cape Sigeum—not far from the tombs of Ajax, Achilles, and Patroclus.

As he quoted from the *Iliad* Alexander solemnly visited the tomb of Achilles. Then, as was the custom, he stripped and ran around it in the nude. Next he visited Troy, the ruins of which are close to Troas—the city where Paul had the vision summoning him to Macedonia.

When he learned about Alexander's invasion, Darius merely shrugged. What could such a whippersnapper do to him? And so the Macedonians marched inland without opposition until they came to the river Granicus where the Persians were lined on the opposite bank. The stream at this place was narrow.

"Let's not attack today," said a Macedonian officer, his eyes on the Persian cavalry of at least 20,000 horses. "This is June, an unlucky month."

"Then turn the calendar back!" shouted Alexander as he rushed forward. "It's now May instead of June!" One glance had convinced the young commander that the Persians had made a grave error. They had crowded their horses so close to the bank it would be impossible for them to maneuver effectively.

Mounted on Bucephalis, Alexander plunged into the churning river. Arrows swished around him. He ignored them. Then a javelin pierced a joint in his breastplate. Next, two Persian generals attacked. One slashed his head with a battle-ax. The ax cut through his helmet. But it stopped at his skull. Then Alexander's spear broke. As sword clashed against sword and spears were blunted by shields, a Persian raised his ax for the final blow. But at that precise moment Cleitus ran the Persian through with his spear.

The Macedonian training and phalanx were too much for the Persians!

The phalanx consisted of 9,000 men. These men were divided into squares with sixteen men on each side. Each man was protected by armor and a thirteen-foot spear. The phalanx could assume various shapes with fantastic precision. It could wheel to the right or the left; assume the shape of a wedge or a pincers. Sometimes the men stood a mere three feet apart. Then, by overlapping the edges of their shields, they formed a living tank. This living tank was so strong wagons could roll over the top of it. It was often mounted by archers so that they could see better when they released their arrows.

Alexander also mastered propaganda. He terrified his enemies by scattering enormous horse-bits where they could be seen easily. This was to give the impression that his cavalry was mounted on a super-breed of horses. He also announced that he was the son of Zeus. But although he claimed divinity, he sacrificed daily to the gods.

Tingling with victory, Alexander strode from triumph to triumph. All callers at his tent had to prostrate themselves before him. Kingdom after kingdom toppled before his advance. Sometimes he won by siege; sometimes by battle. Cities surrendered without struggle. Often he was kind to the defeated. Sometimes not. One of his burning motives was to spread Greek culture across the world.

At Issus, Alexander's handful met the main force of the Persian army of 600,000 under the direct command of Darius III. Again Alexander's foaming horses pushed through to victory.

Damascus and Sidon surrendered quickly. But Tyre—still under the control of Persia—held out. The city had withstood a thirteen-year siege by Nebuchadnezzar; and, with this experience, they felt they could withstand the Macedonians. In preparation for the attack the inhabitants had vacated the "old city" on the mainland and had crowded into the new one on a nearby island. Here the 30,000 defenders were protected by high, thick walls.

Facing this difficulty, Alexander went into council with his commanders. Was Tyre worth the trouble? Why shouldn't they continue east, crush the tottering Persians, and keep going until they had conquered India?

The answer was that Alexander wanted to control Egypt and thus protect Macedonia while he was on his way to India. He was also convinced that he would have to take Tyre before he could take Egypt. This was because both the Tyrenian and Persian fleets remained powerful.

His course set, Alexander built a two-hundred-foot-wide causeway from the mainland to the island. This mole was made by sinking logs from the cedars of Lebanon into the bottom of the sea. It was a gigantic task. The fact that ruins of this causeway still remain indicates his skills.

Tyre surrendered. Eight thousand defenders were slaughtered and 30,000 civilians were sold into slavery. The siege lasted seven months. Alexander celebrated his victory by sacrificing to Hercules in a local temple.

Syria with the exception of Gaza was now in his hands. Gaza resisted. But Alexander's catapults and ladders were too much. The Macedonians poured into the city through a breach in the wall and over the top. All males were killed. Women and children were consigned to slave markets.

Jerusalem surrendered without a struggle.

Egypt, too, collapsed without a fight. Here, Alexander decided to found a new city—Alexandria— on the mouth of the Nile.

Now that he was secure in the Mediterranean, Alexander turned to the east. As before, cities and nations crumbled before his advance. It seemed nothing could stop him. But although he began to adopt Persian ways, at heart he was a Macedonian. He was determined that Greek culture should dominate the world. At Susa Alexander perfected his idea of uniting the Persians and Macedonians. He decided to accomplish this through marriage.

Alexander had already married Roxane, a Persian princess. Now he decided that he would increase the number of interracial marriges. At a gigantic ceremony, Alexander married two new wives: Barsine, eldest daughter of Darius, and Parysatis, youngest daughter of Ochus. Likewise, many of his high officers took Persian brides. Ptolemy married Artcama. Seleucus married the daughter of Spitamenes. In addition, from nine to ten thousand soldiers took Persian wives. When some hesitated because of their debts, Alexander encouraged them to go ahead by personally paying every I.O.U. And to add to his generosity, each couple was presented with a golden cup.

The ceremony cost Alexander nearly a quarter of a billion dollars!

The affair was carried out in lavish splendor. Foreign countries were represented by ambassadors and official delegates. The delegates arrived with wagon loads of gifts.

As a climax to the gigantic wedding, Alexander promised that all children born to these unions would be considered "his kinsmen" and would be educated at the "expense of the state."

Then to add impetus to his goal of Hellenizing the world, Alexander selected thirty thousand of the brightest Persian youths and sent them to Greece to study.

As his conquests progressed Alexander began to get edgy. After the man who had killed Darius was captured, Alexander whipped him almost to death. Then he severed his nose and ears. Next, he sent him to Ecbatana. There, "he was executed by having his arms tied to one, and his legs to the other of two trees that had been drawn together with ropes, so that when the ropes were cut the trees pulled the body to pieces" (*The Life of Greece* by Will Durant).

Alexander was constantly losing his temper. He even attacked friends. It was thus that he killed Cleitus, the man who had saved his life in his first battle with the Persians. Humiliated by what he had done, Alexander began to drink even more heavily. Once he challenged a group of friends to a drinking bout. The prize? A solid gold crown.

Promachus won the bout. But he died three days later—and so did forty-one others.

Dissatisfaction with Alexander began to spread among the troops. Many were convinced that he valued the Persians more than them. Also, they were tired. Eleven years away from home was a long time. Still, Alexander churned with mania to conquer the world. In 327 B.C. he led his men across the lofty Himalayas into India.

Alexander's army crossed the Indus. He defeated King Porus. Then he announced, "Now to the Ganges!" But his men had had enough; and even though he pouted in his tent for three months, the men would not budge. Reluctantly, Alexander began his return home by the way of Babylon.

Early in June while Alexander was inspecting his troops in Babylon, he felt a sudden illness. Convinced he was suffering from the heat, he went for a swim. During his absence, the only ones who remained in his throne room were his eunuchs.

As the eunuchs watched, a stranger stepped inside, walked up to the throne and seated himself. Then he donned Alexander's purple robe and placed the crown on his own head. Because of strict orders, the eunuchs were not allowed to leave their places; and so they contented themselves by tearing their tunics and slapping their foreheads. The man on the throne ignored them.

When Alexander returned he stared, and the intruder stared back. His motionless eyes were as vacant as forgotten caves.

At first Alexander surmised that he was suffering from a hallucination induced by the heat. Then the man on the throne began to speak. "I am from Messenia," he muttered. "My name is Dionysos. I was heaped with chains and unjustly accused. Now I have been delivered by the great god Serapis. This god instructed me to wear the purple and to occupy the throne in silence."

After having the intruder tortured in order to learn if he was telling the truth, Alexander ordered his execution.

The affair was a bad omen.

Soon Alexander's fever—perhaps malaria—began to soar. He died on June 13, 323 B.C. He was not quite thirty-three. Since he had not prepared a will, his vast empire became the spoils of the strongest. Tradition insists that he died in the same room in which Belshazzar perished.

Having spread Greek culture around the Mediterranean world, Alexander the Great helped prepare the way for the advance of Christianity even though he died some three centuries before the coming of Christ. This is so, for Koine Greek became a trade language—spoken throughout many nations in the Mediterranean world.

Chapter 13

Antiochus Epiphanes

Since the Temple in Jerusalem was central in maintaining Jewish determination not to adopt Greek culture, Antiochus Epiphanes determined to ruin it forever. Possessing a sinister brain, and knowing the history of the Jews, Antiochus did not tear down or burn the Temple. No, that would not crush Judaism! The Temple could be rebuilt. His plan was far more drastic than the mere destruction of a building.

Antiochus ordered his troops into Jerusalem; converted the Temple into a shrine for the worship of Jupiter; sacrificed a pig on the altar; sprinkled its blood in the Holy of Holies; cooked a pig—and poured the broth over the Scrolls of the Law. Likewise, he forbade circumcision and any worship of Jehovah. Violators were severely punished. Most were put to death. Mothers who had their sons circumcised were, in several instances, crucified with their sons suspended from their necks on the cross.

To understand these events, we must go back to the death of Alexander the Great in 323 B.C. At that time his hastily assembled empire was divided among his generals. Eventually Seleucus became the ruler of a large section of Asia. Seleucus had been a brilliant officer during all of Alexander's campaigns. Devoted to his father Antiochus, he named sixteen cities after him. And so there were sixteen Antiochs. Only two of these are mentioned in the New Testament: Syrian Antioch and Pisidian Antioch (see Ludwig's *Handbook of New Testament Rulers & Cities*, p. 164. Accent Books).

The empire founded by Seleucus lasted from 312 to 64 B.C. The ruling dynasty was dominated by some of the most corrupt and arrogant tyrants of history. Antiochus I called himself Soter (Saviour); and Antiochus IV—the one in this chapter—assumed the blasphemous title Epiphanes which means God manifest!

All Jews did not refuse to be Hellenized. Many followed the new ways eagerly. It became smart to act and dress like Greeks. With the zeal of an evangelist, each ruler worked to change the thought patterns of the Jews. Gymnasiums were built. Youth were encouraged to compete in the Olympic games. The new ways became more and more popular. Soon, a new generation was speaking Greek and ignoring the Temple.

The Second Book of Maccabees is bitter about such men. "As a result, the priests no longer had any enthusiasm for their duties at the altar, but despised the temple and neglected the sacrifices; and in defiance of the law they eagerly contributed to the expenses of the wrestling-school whenever the opening gong called them. They placed no values on hereditary rights, but cared above everything for Hellenic honors" (II Maccabees 4:14-15, NEB).

Simple country life with its emphasis on farming, three annual pilgrimages to Jerusalem, and a study of the Torah, began to give way to the new vigor. Greek-oriented cities sprang up. These cities had straight wide streets with rows of marble columns; and there were theaters, public baths, and non-Jewish temples. The Greeks emphasized beauty. Moreover, they achieved it. A string of ten of these Greek-dominated cities formed the Decapolis.

These Greek-influenced towns are frequently mentioned in the New Testament. In Mark 5:20 we read: "And he departed, and began to publish in Decapolis how great things Jesus had done for him."

As the Hellenism spread, the rabbis became increasingly hostile. One rabbi even insisted that it was more wicked to speak Greek than to eat pork. Eventually the reaction to this culture produced a society of the pious known as Hasidim. At first, overt clashes were avoided. But the conflict was there, and like cancer cells it kept working.

Antiochus IV did not respond to pressure. His way, he had decided, was *the* way. Many were convinced and listened to him with attentive ears. He liked to dress in ornate robes, crown his head with roses, and swagger through the streets of Antioch. And often as he moved from place to place he handed out gold rings and valuable gems to anyone who happened to especially please him at the moment.

In the beginning, Antiochus did not attack the Jewish faith. But as the rabbis continued their resistance, he turned on them with tiger-like ferocity. He declared that it was illegal to worship Jehovah; abolished the Sabbath; and burned all the copies of the sacred books which his agents could find. The author of First Maccabees described his program in horror-filled lines:

"The king then issued a decree throughout his empire: his subjects were to all become one people and abandon their laws and religion. The nations everywhere complied with the royal command, and many in Israel accepted foreign worship, sacrificing to idols and profaning the sabbath. Moreover, the king sent agents with written orders to Jerusalem and the towns of Judaea. Ways and customs foreign to the country were to be introduced. Burnt-offerings, sacrifices, and libations in the temple were forbidden; sabbaths and feast-days were to be profaned; the temple and its ministers to be defiled. Altars, idols, and sacred precincts were to be established; swine and other unclean beasts to be offered in sacrifice. They must leave their sons uncircumcised; they must make themselves in every way abominable, unclean, and profane, and so forget the law and change all their statutes. The penalty for disobedience was death (I Maccabees 1:43-52, NEB).

Antiochus personally saw to it that his decrees were obeyed. He built pagan altars throughout the land and forced the Jews to worship at them. Next, after he had taken Jerusalem by force of arms he entered the Temple. The story is told in Second Maccabees 5:15-16: "Not satisfied with this, the king had the audacity to enter the holiest temple on earth, guided by Menelaus, who had turned traitor both to his religion and his country. He laid impious hands on the sacred vessels; his desecrating hands swept together the votive offerings which other kings had set up to enhance the splendour and fame of the shrine."

But amidst this turmoil there remained a solid group of the faithful. One of these was an old man by the name of Eleazar who lived in Antioch. Having been seized by the law, he was taken into the presence of Antiochus. (See II Maccabees 6:18-24.)

"It is," said a leader, "the will of the mighty king Antiochus that you eat of the swine meat which has been sacrificed to our god Zeus. If you do the king's bidding your life will be spared, and the king will make you rich and powerful. Should you disobey, our mighty king's command is that you will die a horrible death."

"Silver and gold mean naught to me," replied Eleazar, "and death holds no horrors . . . I will remain faithful to my God and His law to the very day of my death."

The officer admired the old man's spunk and offered to free him if he "would eat meat that is forbidden by your law . . . in front of Zeus and the rest of the people; and the rest of the people, thinking you are eating of the forbidden meat, will follow your example."

When Eleazar continued to refuse, he was tortured to death. This story is one of many—some even more dramatic—that have come from this period.

Adults were not the only ones who suffered. Many recently circumcised babies were slaughtered by Syrian soldiers.

Soon the anger that had seethed beneath the surface for many a year frothed to the top. Secretly and then openly the opposition began to call Antiochus Epiphanes a new name. They dubbed him Antiochus *Epimanes*—the Maniac.

Open rebellion flared in 166 B.C. It was led by an aged priest and his five sons who lived at Modin, a little town some thirteen miles north of Jerusalem. The man's name was Mattathias. Approaching him in the presence of friends, an officer said, "You are a leading man, great and distinguished in this town; now be the first to come forward and carry out the king's command, and you and your sons will be counted among the friends of the king."

Mattathias answered promptly and in a loud voice, "If all the heathen in the king's dominions listen to him and forsake each of them the religion of his forefathers, yet I and my sons and my kinsmen will live in accordance with the Covenant of our forefathers. God forbid that we should abandon the Torah and the ordinances. We will not listen to the king, or depart from our religion to the right hand or to the left."

Mattathias had barely finished when a Jew went up to the altar and began to perform the sacrifice demanded by the king. His heart racing, and being unable to control himself, the old priest killed the man and then the officer. Next, he shouted, "Let everybody who is zealous for the Torah and stands for the Covenant come after me." He then led the way into the mountains. There, he and his friends were soon joined by many members of the Hasidim.

The old man did not live long. But his words continued to flame in people's hearts. Soon his third son, Judas Maccabaeus (perhaps meaning hammer), took up the fight. And, although he was generally outnumbered, he led his men with skill and from victory to victory. Each victory brought new volunteers until soon Judas had a respectable army. Following a triumph at Emmaus and Beth-Zur, Judas felt he was strong enough to subdue Jerusalem and cleanse the Temple. What followed is recorded in the First Book of Maccabees: "So the whole army was assembled and went up to Mount Zion. There the temple laid in waste, the altar profaned, the gates burnt down, the courts overgrown like a thicket . . . They tore their garments, wailed loudly, put ashes on their heads, and fell on their faces to the ground. . . .

"They rebuilt the temple and restored the interior, and consecrated the temple courts. They renewed the sacred vessels and the lampstand, and brought the altar of incense and the table into the temple. When they put the Bread of the Presence on the table and hung the curtains, all their work was completed" (4:17-51, NEB).

On the day of dedication, they eagerly set up the menorah (candelabrum) in order to light the flame that would continue to burn in the Temple. Alas, they found the menorah was dry; and although they searched diligently, they could locate only one jar of sacred oil. That was just enough to burn one night. Nonetheless, according to Jewish historians: "To the great delight of the victorious worshippers . . . a miracle occurred: the small amount of oil lasted eight full days."

And this is the story—perhaps legend—of Hanukkah.

Hanukkah—the Hebrew word means dedication—like the Passover, is filled with long memories for the entire Jewish community. The eight days of Hanukkah fall in December, near Christmas. Although it is not "central in Judaism as Christmas is in Christianity," it is an important festival.

The first candle is lit in the evening of the 25th of Kislev— the anniversary of the day when Judas Maccabaeus entered the Temple. The lighting takes place after the stars are out. Each candle burns only about half an hour, and each day a new candle is lit until all eight of them are burning. The candles are never lit from a match; but rather from a ninth candle which is retained in the extra branch of the candelabrum. This candle is known as the shamesh.

A new Hanukkah tradition has developed in Jerusalem. On the evening of the first night, runners are sent to the village of Modin. There, they kindle a torch from the town's Hanukkah candelabrum. This torch is taken to Jerusalem where it is used to light the candelabrum on the traditional site of King David's tomb on the top of Mount Zion. The torch is then applied to the candelabrums rescued from the Nazi holocaust. Altogether seventy candelabrums—snatched from Auschwitz and other extermination camps—are lit. All of the lighting is done by survivors of the Nazi concentration camps.

It's an impressive sight!

Antiochus Epiphanes was in Persia when he learned that his armies in Judaea were in full retreat. "When the king heard this news, he was thrown into such dismay that he took to his bed, ill with grief at the miscarriage of his plans. There he lay for many days, his bitter grief breaking out again and again, and he realized that he was dying" (I Maccabees 6:8-9, NEB).

After days of agony, and some say remorse, Antiochus Epiphanes died in 163 B.C.

Chapter 14

Measurements, Roads, and Communications

Before we go sniffing down the streets of Old Testament cities, it will be worthwhile to learn the manner in which they were built, how the builders transported their materials, how they kept records and communicated with one another.

The basic concept in all building has to be that of measurement. This is true for the most primitive hut as well as for the tallest skyscraper. The story of measurement is long and curious. Strangely, according to Josephus, the first Biblical person to produce a measuring system was Cain—the world's first murderer. Josephus wrote: "And when Cain had traveled over many countries, he, with his wife, built a city, named Nod . . . He also introduced a change in the way of simplicity wherein men lived before; and was the author of measures and weights. . . ." (*Antiquities of the Jews*).

The oldest recorded unit of length is the cubit. This initial reference is when God instructed Noah that the "length of the ark shall be three hundred cubits. . ." (Genesis 6:7). *This* cubit is assumed to have been the length from the "tip of the elbow to the end of the middle finger." That is, it was about eighteen inches. People's arms, however, are not of the same length. Moreover, this measurement generally accepted in the Mediterranean world, varied from place to place. Egypt alone had three different types of cubits. The oldest was the length of six palms. This cubit was used for household measurements. The second type was the royal cubit. This one consisted of seven palms and was used in planning architecture.

The royal cubit was used in the calculations of the earliest pyramids. "The sides of the Pyramid of Khufu . . . are 440 royal cubits at the base with a mean error in the length of the sides of only one part in 4,000" (*Prepare Now for a Metric Future* by Frank Donavan).

The third cubit used in Egypt was the Ptolemaic cubit. This measurement was slightly different than either of the other two.

As can be logically deducted, our first measurements were derived from the human body. Some of these measurements are still with us. The hand, for example is still used in measuring the height of a horse. Other measurements based on the body are the yard, the foot, and the fathom. The yard evolved from the distance between the tip of a woman's nose and the end of her fingers when her arm is extended. The fathom originated from the space between the tips of a man's fingers when his arms are thrust out horizontally from his body. The foot, of course, was from the length of a human foot.

Nonetheless, if Gertrude Stein had said, a foot is a foot is a foot, she would have been wrong. This is because the length of the foot varied from area to area. A Greek legend insisted that their foot was the exact length of Hercules' foot. If this is correct his foot was an unusually large one. This is so because Plutarch recorded that the width of the main hall in the Parthenon was 100 feet. If we assume he was accurate, Hercules' foot, in comparison to a modern foot was 12.1375 inches long!

The length of a Roman foot was that of Drusus. This "northern" foot was 13.1 inches. On the other hand, the Phoenician foot was a mere 10.98 inches while that of Carthage varied from 11.08 to 11.17 inches.

A system of weights, according to Josephus, also went back to Cain. This system predated the minting of coins. In Genesis 23:16 we read: "And Abraham hearkened unto Ephron; and Abraham weighed to Ephron the silver which he had named in the audience of the sons of Heth, four hundred shekels of silver, current *money* with the merchant."

The weight of the shekel was determined by a certain number of grains—usually of rice or wheat, and sometimes barley. Alas, all shekels were not figured the same way. "It ranged from 120 grains in Palestine to 218 grains in Phoenicia . . . It was not uncommon for a country to have two shekels, one as a monetary standard and the other as a commercial standard; or one weight for internal use and the other for export trade" (*Prepare Now for a Metric Future*).

The earliest builders, of course, learned to use the plumb line; calculate directions from the stars; and determine levels from the position of standing water.

Since the Fertile Crescent was endowed with an excellent river system, Old Testament people made use of rivers for irrigation and for transportation. A thousand years before Abraham, Egyptians had numerous ships and barges on the Nile and were using them efficiently. They transported huge blocks of stone for their building projects. Also, they understood monsoons and sea currents; and were thus enabled to make long voyages across the seas. Queen Hatshepsut, the one who may have rescued Moses from the Nile, had large fleets. Five of her ships went to Punt in Africa and returned with greyhounds, ivory, paint, skins, gold, ebony, and other items.

The Prophet Ezekiel left an excellent description of an ancient ship. "They have made all thy ship boards of fir trees of Senir: they have taken cedars from Lebanon to make masts for thee. Of the oaks of Bashan have they made thine oars; the company of the Ashurites have made thy benches of ivory, brought out of the isles of Chittim. Fine linen with broidered work from Egypt was that which thou spreadest forth to be thy sail; blue and purple from the isles of Elishah was that which covered thee. The inhabitants of Zidon and Arvad were thy mariners: thy wise men, O Tyrus, that were in thee, were thy pilots. The ancients of Gebal and the wise men thereof were in thee thy calkers: all the ships of the sea with their mariners were in thee to occupy thy merchandise" (Ezekiel 27:5-9).

Those ancient mariners did not possess the compass nor modern maps. But they did have an amazing knowledge of at least nearby geography. Also, they knew how to determine directions by the position of mapped landmarks. They also shortened voyages by the use of canals. The present Suez Canal is believed to have followed the approximate course of a previous canal built by a Pharaoh around 500 B.C.

The earliest known record of such a man-made waterway refers to the one used by Queen Hatshepsut: the Red Sea canal. This huge trench stretched from the Egyptian town known as Zagazig across the land of Goshen to Lake Timsah. From there, the ships crossed the Bitter Lake and joined another canal which reached the Red Sea. This useful canal was 16 feet deep and at places 150 feet wide.

Built without explosives or modern machinery, canals were expensive to dig. Herodotus informs us that when Pharaoh Necho attempted to reopen the above canal he faced enormous problems. "A hundred and twenty thousand Egyptians employed on this work ... lost their lives. He at length desisted ... in consequence of an oracle which warned him that he was 'laboring for a barbarian.' " (A barbarian was any person who could not speak Egyptian!) This canal was eventually reopened by Darius. According to Herodotus, it took four days to travel its length.

The better ships used in those days were as nearly advanced as the Mayflower. They even had crow's nests! "Yea, thou shalt be as he that lieth down in the midst of the sea, or as he that lieth upon the top of a mast" (Proverbs 23:34).

All travel could not be done by ship—especially across

deserts. This means they used camels (Genesis 12:16); horses (Genesis 47:17) and mules (II Samuel 13:29). Then, due to dangers on long trips, caravans were used. It was to a caravan that Joseph was sold by his brethren (Genesis 37:25-28).

As the human race advanced and loads became larger, the principle of the wheel was discovered. In our time the principle of the wheel seems extremely simple. And yet there are sections of the world where the wheel was unknown until in the late 1800s of our time! When Alexander Mackay arrived in Uganda in 1878 the natives were astounded by some of the things he possessed: his compass, watch, etc. They were also mystified by his knowledge of the wheel. When they watched this slender missionary roll logs up a hill they were so excited they shouted: "*Mackay lubare! Mackay lubare dala!* Mackay is the great Spirit! Mackay is truly the great Spirit!"

Considering that Uganda at this time was one of the most enlightened countries in Africa, this is amazing. This is so, for they had a navy, a king, manufactured cloth, and sold slaves to the Arabs. Like the American Indians until the advance of the white man, their heavy loads were dragged on sledges.

When was the wheel invented? Our best guess is that it was developed around the fourth millennium B.C. somewhere between the Tigris and Euphrates rivers. The genius who invented it is unknown, but it is believed he was a Sumerian. The oldest sketch of a wheel so far discovered dates back to 3500 B.C. from an account in Sumer. That ancient sketch is of a funeral wagon!

Undoubtedly the first wheel was a solid object, perhaps the slice of a log, with a hole in the center. Across the centuries the wheel improved. About 2000 B.C. some tribes from near the Black Sea suddenly appeared in the Tigris-Euphrates Delta with a huge animal called a horse. Who tamed the horse and developed spokes? Historians shrug. No one knows. But when enemies descended on Egypt with horses and chariots, the Egyptians were quickly subdued. It was thus that the Hyksos period came into being and Joseph became one of the mighty rulers in the land.

The word chariot does not appear in the Old Testament until Genesis 41:43. (See chapter four of this book.)

The wheel continued to slowly improve—especially in the Roman Empire. Having learned that iron expands when it's hot, iron rims came into general use. Nonetheless, there was still the major problem of quick-to-wear-out axles. Then, in the first century B.C. the Danes invented roller bearings. They were made of hard wood and positioned in grooves and caged around the axles.

Curiously, the first example of roller bearings also was found in a funeral wagon!

More efficient ways of travel meant the necessity of better roads. The first Palestinian roads were old cattle trails, dry riverbeds, and paths worn by human beings and then caravans. Eventually, highways came into being. Thus, when Isaiah prophesied that "an highway shall be there" (Isaiah 35:8), he was writing about something which his readers understood. Indeed, there were several well-traveled highways. The Via Maris highway extended from Upper Egypt (Upper Egypt is south and Lower Egypt is north owing to the elevation), through Memphis, Gaza, Megiddo, Tyre, Sidon, Byblos, and up to Ugarit. Another famous route was the King's Highway. This mountainous road connected Damascus with the Gulf of Aqaba. It was known for its roughness, but it was still a very useful road.

Old Testament roads were not of the enduring quality of those built by the Romans just before, during, and after the New Testament era. But sections of some of their roads were substantial. The Cilician Gates, a slit chiseled through heavy rock in the Tarsus Mountains connecting Tarsus to the West, show the use of considerable engineering skill. Xenophon (434 B.C.—355 B.C.) described this shortcut as being a "wagon-road exceedingly steep and impractical for an army to pass."

Nonetheless, it was used! It was through this "gate" that Cyrus the Younger—son of Darius II— led the famed Ten Thousand on their march from Sardis to Babylon in 401 B.C.

As tribes grew numerically larger, cities evolved, and roads were lengthened, the people felt the necessity of finding a way to record events and communicate with others at a distance. This urge led to the invention of writing. Before modern archaeology, it was sometimes assumed that Moses could not have written the Pentateuch for the practical reason that writing had not been invented at the time he lived.

Now, we know that writing had been invented many centuries before the birth of Moses. The Sumerians are credited with the beginnings of pictographic writing—making a sketch of the item to be remembered. This type of writing was limited, for it occupied a lot of space and it was difficult to use in setting down abstract ideas and even indicating the names of cities, people, and thoughts. Moreover, hundreds of different sketches had to be used and memorized.

Pictographic writing soon gave way to cuneiform, and since clay was readily available, it was fashioned into convenient-type slabs and the wedge marks were impressed into the clay. The clay was then baked. Baked slabs were permanent. Tens of thousands of such slabs are preserved in the great museums of the world. Cuneiform was written in all directions: from left to right, from right to left, and even up and down like Chinese.

Soon, other types of writing developed as did also the object on which the writing was inscribed. The Romans became fond of smooth slabs of wax and used a stylus to write on them. A stylus was sharp on one end and flat on the other. The flat end was the "erasure." It could rub out mistakes.

The English word *style* has evolved from this Latin word, stylus.

It has been reported that Caligula—see *Ludwig's Handbook of New Testament Rulers and Cities*—used two types of wax tablets. The black one was used to record the names of those who were to be poisoned; the red one was used to record the names of those who were to be killed with a sword.

The writers of the Bible also wrote on various materials. They wrote on stones, plaster, wood, parchment—an animal skin prepared for writing. Jeremiah 36:23 relates an incident that confirms this. King Jehoiakim sent his secretary "Jehudi to fetch the roll." Then, as the king sat by his fireplace and listened to the secretary as he read "three or four leaves, he cut it with a penknife, and cast it into the fire, until all the roll was consumed in the fire that was on the hearth."

Eventually, papyrus, a seven-foot, triangular plant that thrives on the banks of the Nile in Upper Egypt and elsewhere, took the place of other materials. The thick stem of the papyrus plant is filled with stringy white pulp. The pulp was sliced into thin strips and then laid on a flat surface. Next, more strips, placed at a right angle were laid across the lower ones. These were then beaten with a mallet until they were fused together into a single sheet. This sheet of papyrus had horizontal lines on one side and vertical lines on the other side.

Single sheets of papyrus were sufficient for most normal correspondence. The ink used to write on them was from lampblack mixed with water and the sticky juice from certain plants. (This type of ink was almost completely permanent.)

When more papyrus was needed for a legal document or book, sheets of papyrus were glued together side by side. The usual limit was twenty sheets. After these were filled with writing, they were rolled into a scroll with the horizontal lines on the inside. One scroll was found that was 133 feet long! But the normal scroll was a mere 35 feet from the first sentence to the last. The shortness of the scrolls is one reason some books of the Bible (Kings, Chronicles, and Samuel) were divided into two sections.

Since printing had not been developed in Bible times,

scrolls were reproduced by simply copying them by hand. Indeed, our word manuscript is derived from the Latin *manu scriptum* which means "written by hand." Publishers in that period often dictated books to as many as one hundred slaves at once. It was by this means that bestsellers were kept on the shelves of the booksellers' shops.

Papyrus was cheap; and thus, like modern paper—which word is derived from papyrus—it was often wasted. A record from the third century B.C. relates how a certain Egyptian official made use of 434 papyrus rolls in 33 days!

Copying books was an extremely important work for any Hebrew scribe. Even before he began to copy any Biblical work, he was required to take a ritual bath. The authors of *Ancient Scrolls* have written about this. "No matter how well he [the scribe] knew the passages he was about to copy, he was forbidden to write the text from memory. Instead, he was required to sit with another scroll open before him and to refer to it for each word that he wrote. He was required to take special care of his pen and ink, and he was forbidden to write the four-letter name of God with a pen freshly dipped in ink, lest he make a blot. The space between each word had to be the width of a narrow consonant, and the space between each consonant had to be the width of a human hair! While he was writing, the scribe was required to rid his mind of all distracting thoughts and concentrate on the task before him. In fact, it is written that 'even if he were spoken to by a king, he should not answer' " (Lerner Publications. 1973).

So useful was papyrus, it was still being used for writing by the pope and his secretaries as late as the 11th century A.D. Although many papyrus scrolls perished through fire and dampness, many have survived. Some have even been found inside the mummies of crocodiles! The oldest fragment of the New Testament known to exist is a copy of John 18:31-33, 37-38 which was written on papyrus about A.D. 125. It's in the John Rylands Museum.

Chapter 15

Ur: City of Abraham

On October 26, 1922, a thin, rather shy man picked up a cable form, and after addressing it to a colleague in Philadelphia, wrote in firm, crisp letters: "Expedition starting out."

Leonard Woolley at this time did not know that he was not the first choice of the Committee. All he knew was that he was on his way to Ur of the Chaldees in an expedition sponsored by the British Museum and the University of Pennsylvania. While enroute, he read and reread everything he could find about Abraham.

Few of the passengers on the Mesopotamia-bound ship were impressed by him. A contemporary wrote: "He was a man of slight stature and no commanding appearance. But presence, yes!—and even a blind man would have known what manner of man he was."

Leonard Woolley knew how to get things done!

Before Woolley and his crew began to push their spades into the soil, it was assumed by almost everyone that Ur had been an extremely primitive place. The hot sands surrounding the railway station at Ur—about 120 miles north of Basra near the Persian Gulf—confirmed this assumption. Woolley pulled up his collar for protection against the dust and smiled. The Lord had said to Abraham: "Get thee out of thy country, and from thy kindred, and from thy father's house, unto a land that I will show thee" (Genesis 12:1). Now, as he viewed the sand, Woolley understood why the Lord had issued such a command to his choice son. If he had been in Abraham's place, he would have welcomed such a command! Sand. Everywhere sand. And dirt. Brrr!

But as he worked and studied, Woolley came to the conclusion that Ur had not always been centered in a desert. Indeed, he turned up adequate evidence to prove that four thousand years ago, in the days of Abraham, this had been a very lush country. In that long-ago era the country had been thick with heavily-ladened fig trees, groves of date palms, broad fields of barley and other grains. Also, the land had been laced with a grid of irrigation ditches, and the Euphrates had been heavy with ships exporting surplus commodities. What had caused this drastic change?

Woolley has an explanation. At about the time of Alexander the Great—he died 323 B.C.—"the river Euphrates burst its banks and flowing across the open plain made a new bed for itself more or less where it runs now, eleven miles to the east; and with that change the entire system of water supply was broken up. The old irrigation-canals that had tapped the river further up were left high and dry; the new river course, not yet confined between artificial banks, was a wide lake whose waters, level with the plain, blocked the ends of the drainage-channels so that these became stagnant backwaters: the surface of the plain was scorched by the tropic sun, the subsoil was saturated, and the constant process of evaporation left in the earth such quantities of salt that today irrigation brings to the surface a white crust like hoarfrost which blights all vegetation at birth." (All quotations from Woolley in this chapter are from his book, *Excavations at Ur*.)

After working at Ur for twelve seasons, and after becoming a world-acclaimed archaeologist, Sir Leonard wrote: "We must radically alter our view of the Hebrew patriarch when we see that his early years were passed in such sophisticated surroundings. He was the citizen of a great city and inherited the traditions of an old and highly organized civilization. The houses themselves reveal comfort and even luxury. We found copies of hymns which were used in the services of the temples and together with them mathematical tables. On these were anything ranging from plain addition to sums formulae for the extraction of square and cube root. . . ."

At the time of Abraham's birth, Ur was an old, old city. Some researchers date it back as far as 3200 B.C. If that date is correct, and if Abraham was born about 2166 B.C., as figuring chronology from given Bible facts would indicate, Ur was around 1000 years old when Abraham uttered his first cry!

These intriguing facts about Ur were not known until Woolley proved them to be so in the late 1920s and early 1930s. That they could remain hidden so long is a mystery. This is so because for many centuries it was understood that there were hidden cities beneath the mounds in Mesopotamia.

The story of the mounds is an ancient one. Joshua 11:13 states: "Israel did not burn any cities that stood on their mounds except Hazor. . ." (NASB).

Arabs refer to a mound as a tell or mounds—tulul—and, unlike natural mounds, they are man-made and have flat tops. Mounds have evolved across the centuries. It is interesting how they came into being.

Those who lived in an original city of sun-dried brick, kept their walls repaired by replacing the brick and leaving the crumbled ones out in the street. Likewise, sweepings from the floor and refuse were left nearby. In this manner, the rubble grew higher and higher. Then when the city was burned or forsaken, the next wave of immigrants built their houses on the foundations of the old ones. Thus, across the centuries, mounds came into being like the layers of a cake. A famous mound that demonstrates just how this was done is Tell el-Husn (Mound of the Fortress). This mound has revealed as many as eighteen layers—each representing a separate age.

For many years the Arabs were aware of a high mound about 120 miles north of Basra and about 10 miles west of the Euphrates. They named it Tell el-Maqayyar (Mound of Pitch), but no one did anything to investigate it. To the natives or occasional travelers, it was just a useless, reddish stump fit for the inhabitation of owls.

But unable to contain his curiosity, J. E. Taylor, British vice-consul in Basra in 1854, organized a crew, mounted the top—and began to excavate. Being untrained, he was ruthless and did a lot of damage. While his crew was digging and tossing brick and broken tile down the sides, the workers suddenly discovered some little bars with cuneiform writing on them.

Delighted, Taylor shipped the bars to the British Museum where they were promptly forgotten. After all, why should they be interested? The intense interest at that time was in the excavations at Khorsabad and Nineveh, four or five hundred miles to the north.

Now that the mound was opened, those who wanted building materials simply helped themselves. The fact that the bricks were marked with the names of Ur-Nammu or Nabonidus meant nothing to them. In their minds a brick was a brick even though it had been made 4,000 years ago!

Tell el-Maqayyar kept getting shorter and shorter as the years went by. Then in 1918, with the British in control at Baghdad, Captain R. Campbell Thompson took time off from his regular work to investigate the remains of the stump. Fortunately, during peacetime, he had worked for the British Museum, thus he had a trained eye and understood the value of ancient bricks, pieces of pottery, and so forth. Excited by what he was finding, Thompson sent urgent messages to the British Museum. These messages prompted a study of the bars and tablets which Taylor had dispatched in 1854.

As the tablets were studied, it became evident that Taylor was not the first to push a shovel into the mound. No, another had done so in the sixth century B.C.—about 2500 years before. This previous "archaeologist" had been none other than Nabonidus, a king of Babylon and the father of Belshazzar, the king whose knees thumped! Inspired by the importance of this mound—it turned out to be a ziggurat—Nabonidus had decided to repair it. "I restored this ziggurat to its former state with mortar and bricks," he boasted.

The British Museum now discovered that some of the tablets forwarded by Taylor had stamped on them the names of Ur-Nammu and his son Dungi. Likewise, it was discovered Nabonidus had placed his own imprint on many bricks.

The name Ur-Nammu electrified the world. This is because Genesis 11:31 reads: "And Terah took Abram his son, and Lot the son of Haran his son's son, and Sarai his daughter-in-law, his son Abram's wife; and they went forth with them from Ur of the Chaldees, to go into the land of Canaan; and they came unto Haran, and dwelt there."

The almost breathless scholars asked: "Is there a connection between Ur-Nammu and Ur of the Chaldees?" Today, most scholars agree there definitely is! Ur-Nammu was simply one of the kings who ruled around 2112 B.C. during the Third Dynasty of Ur. Thus, the eighteen-year rule of this king was during the years Abraham was residing in Ur.

Now we know that the Ur-Nammu ziggurat—Tell el Maqayyar—occupied much of the city that Abraham knew. Ziggurats—the name means pinnacle—were being built in Mesopotamia long before the pyramids were erected in Egypt. Sir Leonard has left a description: "In form the ziggurat is a stepped up pyramid having three stages . . . The lowest stage (of the one at Ur) is well preserved, measures at ground level 200 feet in length by 150 feet in width and is about fifty feet high; from this rose the upper stages, each smaller than the one below, leaving broad passages along the main sides and wider terraces at either end; on the topmost stage stood the little one-roomed shrine to the Moon-god, the most sacred building in Ur, for whose setting the whole of this vast substructure had been planned.

"On three sides the walls rose sheer to the level of the first terrace . . . Three brick stairways, each of a hundred steps, led upwards. . . ." Those steps led to the shrine at the top.

Woolley was intrigued with the ziggurat; but he was also concerned with the several mounds nearby. Could it be that they covered the city of Ur?

Early in 1923 Woolley and his workers began to open a mound just east of the ziggurat. With excitement similar to that experienced by Moses at the Burning Bush, they were extremely careful with their picks and each handful of soil. But each day ended in disappointment. And this disappointment continued for six winters. Then in the spring of 1929 they began to be rewarded with significant discoveries. The first of these was a series of five temples, the largest of which was 300 feet in length by 180 feet in width.

The largest temple had been dedicated to the Moon-god. The entire area was amazingly complete. Old fountains and water troughs were still intact, as were the ovens where the sacrificial animals were prepared in the kitchen temples. Deeply moved by his discoveries, Sir Leonard wrote: "After 3800 years we were able to light a fire again and put into commission once more the oldest kitchen in the world."

Further excavation revealed villas with thirteen and fourteen rooms in which the ground floor was made of burned brick and the upper story of sun-dried brick. There were stone staircases, inside lavatories, beautiful mosaics, exquisite jugs, vases, and small tablets.

Signs of a significant civilization were everywhere.

A workshop was unearthed where twelve different kinds of clothing were manufactured. They even found lists of the names of the girls who were employed there. But that was not all. Quotas of wool were also noted as well as the production of each worker!

Woolley became so accustomed to the buildings in the unearthed city, and having read many of the names of the occupants in cuneiform, he often led visitors through the ruins and remarked as they walked along, "This is where _____ lived. And this was the home of _____. This man must have been a businessman, for we found lists of his customers. Over there was the home of a man who was obviously in the export business. We know that by the number of foreign objects we found lying around."

As Woolley and his men worked, many world celebrities came to watch. And since he was an expert at getting publicity, his discoveries were constantly making headlines.

The discovery of Ur proved that Abraham was not an illiterate nomad; but rather a sophisticated person, used to luxuries that were unknown even in Babylon a thousand years later. Nonetheless, it was also discovered that the inhabitants of Ur were confirmed idolators and that they even indulged in human sacrifices. Woolley's thorough examination of the remains in several cemeteries proved this. He wrote:

"The best example of the 'death-pit' was that of our royal grave PG/1237; the tomb chamber had been completely destroyed by robbers, but the 'death-pit' was intact . . . The pit measured, at the bottom, twenty-seven feet by twenty-four . . . Six men-servants carrying knives or axes lay near the entrance . . . Over the rest of the pit's area there lay in ordered rows the bodies of sixty-four ladies of the court. All of them wore some sort of ceremonial dress; a few threads and patches preserved by being in contact with stone or metal showed that this had included a short-sleeved coat of scarlet, the cuffs enriched with beadwork in lapis lazuli, carnelian and gold, with sometimes a belt of white shell rings; it may have been fastened in the front with a long pin of silver or copper; round the neck was worn a "dog-collar" of lapis lazuli and gold together with other looser necklaces of gold, silver, lapis lazuli and carnelian beads; in the ears were very large crescent-shaped earrings of gold or silver and twisted spirals of gold or silver wire kept in order the curls above the ears. The headdress was much like that of Queen Shub-ad; a long ribbon of gold or silver was looped several times round the hair and, at any rate with those of higher rank, a triple band of gold, lapis lazuli and carnelian beads were fastened below the ribbon with gold beech-leaf pendants hanging across the forehead. Twenty-eight of these court ladies wore golden hair-ribbons, the rest silver. . . ."

What was the explanation of this orderly grave? Simple. The queen had died and her guards along with her court attendants had dressed in their finest, taken their places in the pit, and had been buried alive with the corpse of the queen. The purpose of this was so that they could attend her in the next life.

This burial-pit was a great discovery. But Sir Leonard was disappointed. This was because the bodies and ornaments were not in good condition. He explained: "Unfortunately silver is a metal which ill resists the action of acids in the soil, and where it was but a thin strip, and being worn on the head, was directly affected by the corruption of the flesh, it generally disappears altogether, and at the most there may be detected on the bone of the skull slight traces of a purplish color which is silver chloride in a minutely powdered state: we could be certain that the ribbons were worn, but we could not produce material evidence of them."

Then Sir Leonard had the great fortune of discovering one body that had remained in moderately good condition. "The gold earrings were in place, but not a sign of discoloration betrayed the evidence of any silver headdress . . . then as the body was cleared, there was found against it, about on the level of the waist, a flat disck of a little more than 3 inches across the grey substance which was certainly silver; it might have been a small circular box. Only when I was cleaning it in the house that evening, hoping to find something that would enable me to catalogue it in more detail, did its real nature come to light: it was the silver hair-ribbon, but it had not been worn. . . ."

Why hadn't it been worn? Probably because the lady had

not had time to completely prepare for her own funeral. One can easily imagine the final drama:

"You'd better hurry, all the others are in place; the mourners are getting impatient, and the grave-diggers are anxious to fill up the grave so that they can go home."

Unable to complete her toilet, the lady put the ribbon in her pocket, leaped into the pit, and patiently waited to be buried alive.

It was because of this background, together with the call of the Lord, that seventy-five-year-old Abraham assembled his family and left this ancient city of the past in order to migrate to a new country which the Lord would show him.

Chapter 16

Nineveh: City of Mystery

In our time, Nineveh is only a memory. But three thousand years ago it was one of the most powerful and respected cities on earth. Its ultimatums made kings tremble. Tracing its story leads one from one mystery to another. Its history is wrapped in hard-to-understand paradox. Even so, the puzzle is being slowly assembled; and, as additional evidence becomes available, that evidence makes the trustworthiness of the Bible more and more apparent.

Nineveh was one of the oldest large cities in the world.

The record of Nineveh's beginnings are recorded in Genesis 10:11-12. "From that land [Shinar] he [Nimrod] went forth into Assyria [Asshur] and built Nineveh. . ." (vs. 12, NASB).

Nimrod, of course, was the man described in Genesis 10:9 as "a mighty hunter before the Lord." Nimrod was a son of Cush who was a son of Ham. Thus, Nimrod was a great-grandson of Noah!

The land where these events took place was in the area which the ancients called Mesopotamia—"land between the rivers." These rivers are the Tigris and the Euphrates. The 1700-mile-long Euphrates rises in the mountains of eastern Turkey and flows southwestward into the Persian Gulf. Only 25 miles shorter than the Danube, it is one of the world's great rivers and drains an area about the size of Texas. The smaller and more shallow Tigris is just east of the Euphrates and winds in approximately the same direction toward the Persian Gulf. The 1150-mile Tigris has shifted its course during the last hundreds of years. At one time it joined the Euphrates at Korna. Now the two rivers meet at Garmat Ali and flow together as the Shatt al Arab into the Persian Gulf.

Shaped like a huge exclamation point with a bulge in the center and the Persian Gulf as the dot, ancient Mesopotamia had an area of 143,000 square miles—the approximate combined area of the states of Ohio, Pennsylvania, and New York.

Today, much of this country is in northern Iraq.

The Biblical Garden of Eden was somewhere within this region, although no one has yet been able to prove its precise location. Nonetheless, it seems evident that Mesopotamia was the cradle of the human race as well as that of the horse, ox, sheep, goat, dog, and other domesticated animals. Also it was here that such products as figs, dates, cherries, apples, oats, barley, peas, and beans began to grow. Likewise, this area produced the wheel and the game of chess. This game was being played as far back as 4000 B.C.

Nineveh was built on the east side of the Tigris just across from the modern Iraq city Mosul.

The river Khoser which was eventually used by the enemy to destroy Nineveh, flowed eastward from the Tigris through the city. With these two rivers, plus a canal which was constructed to carry water from the Tigris to the edge of the city's western wall, there was plenty of water for moats, fountains, irrigation, and household use.

From 1100 B.C. Nineveh was a royal residence. Then, during the reign of Sargon II (722-705 B.C.), it served as the capital of Assyria. Sennacherib (705-681 B.C.) especially loved Nineveh. He made it his royal residence and the main city of his empire. This is confirmed in the Biblical account: "So Sennacherib king of Assyria departed, and went and returned, and dwelt at Nineveh" (II Kings 19:36).

Sennacherib made many improvements in Nineveh. He had ordered massive walls to be constructed. These were two and a half miles long between the city and the Tigris, and eight miles long around the rest of the city. He also built the oldest aqueduct in history. This water carrier was of masonry construction. It was 1000 feet long and 80 feet wide. It was part of a canal which brought water from the mountains thirty-five miles away.

Such improvements cost money. But, being a conqueror, Sennacherib had no great problem in raising money. A great deal came from tribute. Biblical accounts of these tribute revenues are found in II Kings 15:20, 18:31; Jeremiah 50:17; Isaiah 8:4; and Hosea 10:6.

The precise age of Nineveh is unknown. But we do know that it is referred to in Babylonian records that extend back to the 21st century B.C. Likewise, it was mentioned in the records of Hammurabi who ruled between 1792 and 1750 B.C. We can, however, be more precise about the city's destruction. This is because of Biblical and historical accounts.

The prophet Nahum became lyrical about Nineveh's destruction. In the book that bears his name, he wrote: "Woe to the bloody city! it is all full of lies and robbery . . . The noise of a whip, and the noise of the rattling of the wheels, and the pransing horses, and of the jumping chariots" (3:1-2). "And it shall come to pass, that all they that look upon thee shall flee from thee, and say, Nineveh is laid waste: who will bemoan her? whence shall I see comforters for thee?" (vs. 7). Then in verse 19 he ends with a mighty clap: "There is no healing of thy bruise; thy wound is grievous: all that hear the bruit [news] of thee shall clap the hands over thee: for upon whom hath not thy wickedness passed continually?"

Zephaniah also wrote bitterly about Nineveh and its coming demise: "And he will stretch out his hand against the north, and destroy Assyria; and will make Nineveh a desolation, and dry like a wilderness. And flocks shall lie down in the midst of her, all the beasts of the nations: both the cormorant and the bittern shall lodge in the upper lintels of it; their voice shall sing in the windows; desolation shall be in the thresholds. . ." (2:13-14).

The bitterness of Zephaniah over the coming destruction of Nineveh is easily explained. Sargon II (Isaiah 20:1) who lived between 722 and 705 B.C., had conquered Samaria and deported 27,290 of her citizens. Sargon's son, Sennacherib, ascended the throne in 705 B.C. and ruled until his assassination in 681 B.C. Like his father, he attacked Israel and demanded heavy tribute from Hezekiah (II Kings 18:13-16).

Nineveh had become arrogant, cruel, bloodthirsty. An Assyrian relief carries the words of Esarhaddon, one of her kings: "I hung the heads of Sanduarri and of Abdimilkutte round the necks of their nobles . . . to demonstrate to the population the power of Ashur, my lord, and paraded thus through the wide main street of Nineveh with singers [playing on] . . . harps" (*Nineveh and the Old Testament* by Andre Parrot).

A cuneiform tablet deciphered in 1923 helps us pinpoint the date of the fall of Nineveh. After a siege by a combined force made up of Medes, Scythians, and Babylonians, it fell in August, 612 B.C. The king and many of his officers were killed during this attack.

The end was brought by opening the gates of the Khoser River and allowing it to flow into the city where it dissolved the sun-dried brick. This was a remarkable fulfillment of Nahum's prophecy: "The gates of the rivers shall be opened, and the palace shall be dissolved" (Nahum 2:6). Zephaniah's prediction about the city's desertion (2:14-15) also came to pass. Indeed, Nineveh was utterly blotted out for 2000 years.

Two centuries after Nineveh's collapse, the Greek soldier and historian, Xenophon, joined Cyrus the Younger in 401 B.C. Together with the famed 10,000 they passed Nineveh by the way of a dry riverbed on their way to the Black Sea. But although Xenophon mentioned seeing the remains of a quay which he mistakenly believed to be part of the wall of ancient Larsa, he never mentioned Nineveh.

NINEVEH

In the twelfth century A.D., an educated Jew, Benjamin Tudela, wrote: "This city [Mosul] situated on the Tigris, is connected with ancient Nineveh by a bridge . . . Nineveh lies now in utter ruins, but numerous villages and small towns occupy its former space."

The mysterious city of Nineveh did not come to public notice until the ruins were positively identified by Henry Layard on December 22, 1853. Although not an archaeologist, Layard's discoveries at Nineveh were so substantial, he became known as the Father of Assyriology. In our time, as one views the artifacts he sent to the British Museum, one has to agree that his title was well deserved. A grateful public elected him to the House of Parliament, Oxford gave him an honorary degree, and he received a knighthood.

To moderns, the most famous person connected with the drama at ancient Nineveh was Jonah. Controversy has swirled about this man, especially during the last two centuries. Much of this is due to the three days which he spent in the "great fish" which swallowed him. The book of Jonah does not call the fish a whale, but today we know that there are sperm whales in the Mediterranean with gullets large enough to swallow a man.

That Jonah, "the son of Amittai" really existed is a fact. (Jonah, also Jonas and Jona, come from a Greek word for dove.) He is referred to in II Kings 14:11 where we are told that he was from Gath-hepher. This is less than five miles northwest of Nazareth!

Having been called to go to Nineveh, Jonah sailed for "Tarshish." When the Tarshish-bound ship was about to sink because of a storm, Jonah suggested that they throw him overboard. This they did with great reluctance. After three days and nights the fish "which the Lord had prepared" vomited him out on dry land. He then proceeded to Nineveh.

The Book of Jonah, the author of which we assume to be

Jonah, never refers to a person or thing which might provide a clue as to a date. He doesn't even name the king. He simply refers to him as "the king of Nineveh" (3:6).

Since Jonah is mentioned, however, as a prophet during the reign of Jeroboam II who reigned from 786 to 746 B.C., we can assume that his journey to Nineveh took place during this period (see II Kings 14:23-25).

A problem that has puzzled scholars is that the author speaks of Nineveh as being "an exceeding great city of three days' journey" (3:3). This is a difficulty because the city's 45 to 50 foot high wall was only twelve miles in circumference; moreover, a city that small could hardly contain, at least not comfortably, "sixscore thousand persons" (Jonah 4:11).

One solution might be that Jonah was probably thinking of Nineveh and its suburbs. These might have included Khorsabad, ten miles to the north, and Calah, twenty miles to the south.

Did Nineveh repent? So far there have been no archaeological confirmations. Nonetheless, we are confident that evidence will be found that will prove she did. The natives of Iraq confirm the story of Jonah and are eager to point out his grave to tourists. This grave, only a short distance from Nineveh, is called *Tell Nabi Younis*—the Hill of the Prophet Jonah. Moreover, Jesus stated that Nineveh repented, and that's all the evidence we need. (See Matthew 12:41.)

When Layard unearthed Nineveh, he discovered the priceless library of Ashurbanipal—the last great king of Assyria (669-626 B.C.). From the colophon attached to the cuneiform tablets in this library, it was learned that he was probably the world's first "book" collector. That colophon reads: "The wisdom of Nebo in the writing of every kind, in tablets I wrote, collated, and revised, and for examination and reading in my palace I placed."

The tablets in this library, inscribed with cuneiform, vary in size from a square inch to as much as 15 x 8 1/2 inches. These "books," about 25,000 of them, were sent to the British Museum where they can now be seen. They include dictionaries, prayers, contracts, and works on law, history, and geography. In them one can read the story of the flood during the years of Noah.

This library has verified many of the disputed accounts in the Bible. Likewise, it has added insights. For example, here is part of the Assyrian version of II Kings 18:13-16: "Now in the fourteenth year of king Hezekiah did Sennacherib king of Assyria come up against the fenced cities of Judah, and took them. And Hezekiah king of Judah sent to the king of Assyria to Lachish, saying, I have offended; return from me: that which thou puttest on me I will bear . . . At that time did Hezekiah cut off the gold from the doors of the temple of the Lord, and from the pillars which Hezekiah king of Judah had overlaid, and gave it to the king of Assyria" (this translation is from *Guide to The Babylonian and Assyrian Antiquities*, published by the British Museum in 1922).

The world owes a great debt to Layard. Because of him, we can go to the British Museum and study many of the great monuments of Assyria. Few who casually view them, however, realize the sweat and agony Layard spent in order to secure them. While digging into mounds, the local authorities did all they could to hinder him. One of their techniques was to place fake gravestones over a mound and then insist that he was digging into a cemetery!

One afternoon the governor's representative made a confession: "We have destroyed more real tombs of the true believers in making sham ones than you could have defiled between the Zab and Selamiyah. We have killed our horses and ourselves in carrying those accursed stones" (*The Bible and Archaeology* by Sir Frederic Kenyon).

After visiting a chief, Layard was on his way back to the mound he was excavating when two of his men, riding on horses at full speed, rode up. "We have just made a wonderful find," their leader panted.

Following their lead, Layard stopped at the trench where they were working. There, he saw a huge statue—perhaps a human-headed bull or lion. While he stood in awe, the Arab chief along with perhaps half of his tribe, approached.

The chief glanced at the object, and then he sneered: "This is not the work of men's hands, but of those infidel giants of whom the Prophet (peace be with him!) has said that they were higher than the tallest date-tree. This is one of the idols which Noah (peace be with him!) cursed before the Flood" (*The Bible and Archaeology*).

By a series of miracles, Layard managed not to antagonize the local population to the point where they would stop him. His new find turned out to be a huge, human-headed lion. This magnificent piece of art was one of a pair that guarded a chamber leading into the palace. Today it glowers benignly at viewers from a choice spot in the British Museum.

It's worth a trip to London just to see it!

Chapter 17

Goshen: Land of Mystery

Although the drama is over thirty-five hundred years old, lasted for almost half a millennium, had many acts, and used many stage settings, the names of some of the principal actors cannot be recalled with precision—and the setting of some of its finest action can only be approximated.

The drama is the story of Joseph and his brethren. The lost setting is the land of Goshen where the drama reached a climax when Moses achieved permission for the Exodus.

But before we peer into the land of Goshen, let's go back to the pit where Joseph had been tossed at the suggestion of his brother Reuben. Miraculously, instead of leaving him there where he would have starved, the brothers sold him to some Midianite merchantment for twenty pieces of silver. These merchants then took Joseph to Egypt. That is the end of Act I.

In Egypt, due to the fact that the Hyksos were in command, Joseph quickly became a power in government. At his suggestion, storage bins were built and filled with grain in preparation for the famine Joseph knew would grip the land. Following seven years of plenty, Egypt's storage facilities were overflowing. Then famine came and it extended into Canaan where Joseph's father Jacob and his brethren were living. Soon the hungry began to make their way to Egypt to buy grain; and among the hungry were Joseph's brethren.

Act II relates how Joseph's father, one-hundred-and-thirty-year old Jacob, and his brethren and their families moved to Egypt. Being a man of influence, Joseph persuaded Pharaoh to allow his father and other relatives to move into the land of Goshen. But where was Goshen?

Genesis 46:29 provides a hint in regard to its location. That famous passage reads:

> And Joseph made ready his chariot, and went up to meet Israel [Jacob] his father, to Goshen, and presented himself unto him; and he fell on his neck, and wept on his neck a good while.

Since Joseph went to meet his father, it would seem obvious that he went in an easterly direction. Another passage that gives a hint about its location is Genesis 47:5,6:

> And Pharaoh spake unto Joseph saying, Thy father and thy brethren are come unto thee: The land of Egypt is before thee; in the best of the land make thy father and brethren to dwell; in the land of Goshen let them dwell: and if thou knowest any men of activity among them, then make them rulers over my cattle.

Those words prove three things: Goshen was in the land of Egypt. Goshen was in the best land. (This means it was on the banks of the Nile.) And it was excellent land for cattle grazing. With these facts as a guide, most researchers agree that this land was in lower Egypt in the lush Nile Delta.

The land of Goshen had an area of about 900 square miles. That is, it was about four-fifths the size of Rhode Island. It extended from Lake Timsah on the Nile, was centered in Wadi Tumilat and was from forty to fifty miles long.

All went well for the sons of Jacob in the land of Goshen. The people prospered "and increased abundantly, and multiplied, and waxed exceeding mighty; and the land was filled with them" (Exodus 1:7). But problems followed, for Joseph had died; the Egyptians had defeated the Hyksos, "and there arose up a new king over Egypt who knew not Joseph" (vs. 8).

Having been crushed and ruled by the mysterious Hyksos, the Egyptians were suspicious of anyone who might repeat what they had done. Their suspicions focused on the children of Israel. This is the end of Act III.

Without naming him, Moses outlined the character of the new ruler: "And he said unto his people, Behold the people of the children of Israel are more and mightier than we: Come on, let us deal wisely with them; lest they multiply, and it come to pass, that, when there falleth out any war, they join also unto our enemies, and fight against us, and so get them up out of the land. Therefore they did set over them taskmasters to afflict them with their burdens. And they built for Pharaoh treasure cities, Pithom and Raamses" (Exodus 1:9).

Each treasure or store city had a colorful name. According to some, Pithom means "their mouthful." Raamses means "child of the sun." Their location is in dispute. But most researchers believe they were in the land of Goshen. One guess is that Pithom is located at Tell el-Retabeh and Raamses at Tanis. Both of these ruins are within a few miles of each other.

The major task of the Israelites in both of these places was to make sun-dried brick. Harsh taskmasters with ready whips stood nearby as they worked, and any pause brought the whip down on naked shoulders. But in spite of the hard work, the children of Abraham continued to multiply. Eventually, Pharaoh ordered that they cast brick without straw. The results of this are now pointed out to tourists at the ruins of Pithom. An old wall stands there which has normal straw-lined brick in the bottom rows, rows filled with stubble higher up, and completely strawless brick at the top.

Working without straw and working from sunup until sundown did not stop the people from multiplying. In desperation, Pharaoh ordered the male children drowned. All of this led to the call of Moses, the many plagues, and finally Pharaoh's permission for them to leave. The exact route of the Exodus is hard to determine. But most scholars agree that they departed from the land of Goshen.

That the land of Goshen was a fertile place is indicated by the way some of the people complained as they trekked toward the Promised Land. Part of their complaint is recorded in Numbers 11:4-6. "Who will give us flesh to eat? We remember the fish, which we did eat in Egypt freely; the cucumbers, and the melons, and the leeks, and the onions, and the garlick: But now our soul is dried away: there is nothing at all, beside this manna, before our eyes."

For years unbelievers have tried to discount the Biblical story about the Israelites in Egypt, the birth of Moses, and the Exodus. One of their arguments is that Egypt is not filled with monuments testifying to these events. Such critics forget that the Egyptians were not in the business of glorifying their failures. They did not build a monument in honor of either the Hyksos or Moses. Our tallest monument is in honor of George Washington, not George III!

Nonetheless, there are archaeological evidences in Egypt that the Hebrews were there. A relief in Memphis, dating back to the 14th century B.C., shows Semite captives and their Egyptian guard. A painting in a vault shows light-skinned men dressed only in aprons, both making and laying brick. A guard with a darker skin and armed with a rod sits nearby and a hieroglyphic sign says, "The rod is my hand. Be not idle."

A stele discovered in Thebes features a poem:

> Wasted is Tehenu [a tribe on the
> Libyan border of Egypt],
> The Hittite land is pacified,
> Plundered is Canaan with every evil,

> Carried off is Askalon,
> Seized upon is Gezer;
> Yenoam is made as a thing not
> existing,
> Israel is desolated, her seed is not,
> Palestine has become a defenceless
> widow for Egypt.
>   (Quoted from *The Bible and Archae-
> ology* by Sir Frederic Kenyon.)

Another relief, this one from the tomb of Rameses III, shows a line of slaves who were working for the Egyptians. The first in the line is obviously a Libyan. Then follows a Semite, Hittite, and Philistine.

One of the great miracles experienced by the children of Israel is that during their more than four hundred years in Egypt, they retained their own language, their own faith, and their own culture. Surely this demonstrates the power of the Lord!

Chapter 18

Thebes: City of Tombs

In his gallery of the faithful, the author of the Book of Hebrews used a mere eighteen words to express one of the great facts known to the human race. Inspired by the Holy Spirit, he wrote: "By faith Moses, when he was come to years, refused to be called the son of Pharaoh's daughter" (Hebrews 11:24).

Those words, refused to be called the son of Pharaoh's daughter, throb with life. How was that possible?

Raised in a palace, living in the midst of unbelievable luxury, enjoying the advantages of an excellent education, Moses surely must have been tempted to remain in an easy chair, live on gourmet food, and exclaim, "This is the life for me!" Instead, accelerated by great purpose, his heart remained firmly with his people—slaves though they were.

In order to understand the tremendous gap that existed between Moses and his Hebrew relatives, let's slip by a gang of the Hebrews working under the whip at Pithom or Raamses, board a ship, sail up the Nile, and check into a hotel in Thebes—a city in which Moses undoubtedly visited many times. Indeed, as we have suggested, he may have attended school there, for it was a center of learning.

The trip *up* the Nile on the way south is a rather long one—at least four hundred miles. And since, contrary to most rivers, it flows northward, the trip takes a long time. If, when we boarded the ship we had said that we were going to Thebes, we would have met with blank stares. This is because Thebes is a rather new name, bestowed on the city by the Greeks. During the days of Moses, the place was called *Waset*, "the Scepter." However, due to its magnificence, others dubbed it "The City." And still others referred to it as the "City of Amun." Amun was one of its best known gods.

Thebes, like New York City with its Bronx, Yonkers, Brooklyn, Manhattan, and so on, had various sections. These included Karnak, popularly referred to as Ipet-Isut "Most-Select-of-Places;" and Luxor, shrugged at as "The Southern Sanctuary." (Sanctuary meant harem!)

During its prime, Thebes, including its suburbs, stretched for a long nine miles on the banks of the Nile.

Egyptians who were privileged to visit Thebes did so with a sense of pride; for, it was their *great* city, and it was a place of distinction. During the Hyksos occupation, Thebes had been practically free most of the time. Indeed, the force that threw the Hyksos out of Egypt was centered there.

But, although Thebes was a city of palaces, temples, museums, obelisks, restaurants, beautiful streets, and places of business, it was a dirty city. There were some inside toilets. But, nevertheless, the wastes ended up outside. Often on the streets. This waste produced flies. Millions and millions of flies. No one carried umbrellas. Instead, almost everyone was equipped with a fly whisk. In a well-known tomb-painting, the king's number one wife is shown with a fly whisk in her hand. Flies, however, were not the only problem.

Thebes stretched out on the *Black Land*—the fertile miles that bordered the Nile; still, dust from the *Red Land*—the desert—was constantly clouding the city. It blew through windows, seeped into closets, filled lungs, soiled the streets, fogged the air. In addition, there were poisonous snakes, gnats, lice, fleas, scorpions, mice, rats, jackals—and occasionally locusts.

The wharfs were loud with the songs—and curses—of

workers who loaded and unloaded ships. Chained slaves spoke numerous languages as they pushed wagons, swept streets, cultivated the soil. Long barges loaded with stone blocks and grain moved up and down the river, and ships that had been across the *Great Green* to Africa and even India unloaded their wares: silks, curious animals, spices, exotic perfumes, rouge for eyes and lips. The poor shuffled down the streets in sandals. The rich rode in elaborately built chariots. Royalty had chariots inlaid with precious stones, decorated with ornaments, and covered with gold. It was the aim of the pharaohs to have such dazzling chariots that when they were whisked down the streets the people were reminded of the approach of the sun.

Before Moses became a fugitive at the age of forty he was treated with great respect. After all, he had been raised by Pharaoh's daughter—probably Hatshepsut, daughter of Thutmose I, half-sister and wife of Thutmose II, and aunt of Thutmose III. With this background, Moses never became a slave. Instead, he was a member of the elite class. Slow of speech though he was, a word from him sent servants scrambling to fulfill his every wish. This is indicated in Exodus 2:11, "And it came to pass in those days, when Moses was grown, that he *went out*, unto his brethren, and looked on *their* burdens: and he spied an Egyptian smiting an Hebrew, one of his brethren" (italics mine). The words "their" and "went out" indicate the high position he enjoyed.

Tall, sharp cliffs on the west side of the river rose high and straight up like the remainder of a cake that had been sliced in two. In this treeless area there were "hidden" places where previous pharaohs had been buried. It had been the hope of each that the professional grave-robbers would never find his grave. Alas, almost all of them had hoped for the impossible. Houses of craftsmen that shared common walls also honeycombed the west side. These houses, built of sun-dried brick, with mud-plastered walls, intermingled with homes of those who built tombs, chariots, furniture.

Many of these workers were extremely fine craftsmen. They could make wooden joints so fine the joining could hardly be seen. Indeed, their chairs and tables would rival the finest chairs and tables built in the Western world in our time.

The elite in Thebes, however, lived in utter extravagance. They paid little attention to the homes of the workers. They spent their time hunting, banqueting, fulfilling the desires of the flesh, reading, dancing, plotting new buildings, playing checkers and other games. The wealthy enjoyed the antics of jugglers, acrobats and storytellers. One pharaoh boasted that he had killed over one hundred lions.

Many kitchens were dominated by several cooks, each a specialist. One cook prepared meats, another cakes, another breads. A single papyrus cookbook has forty recipes for cakes. The people especially enjoyed the shat cake. It was made of date flour and honey and was fried. Strangely, no one had developed an oven.

The poor lived on such staples as vegetables, dates, eggs, melons, grapes—and products of flour. Fish, too, were popular.

Each pharaoh tried to erect more statues and buildings in his own honor than those of his predecessors. Also, many of them tried to destroy, desecrate, or at least alter the monuments of those they followed. Hatshepsut had a passion in ordering obelisks and magnificent stone likenesses of herself. In some of these, her face replaced the face of a lion stretched out on a pedestal.

Today, the tallest obelisk in Egypt is that of Hatshepsut. It stands in Karnak, is 97½ feet tall, and weighs 323 tons. An inscription insists that it was cut "from one block of hard red granite without any patches or flaws." A line on it from the queen herself indicates some of her pride. She wrote: "Let not him who hears this say, 'It is a lie!' . . . but rather let him say, 'How like her who is truthful in the sight of her father [Amun]!' "

The largest obelisk ever attempted still lies in a granite quarry at Aswan. This one is 137 feet long, 14 feet wide at the base, and weighs 1200 tons. It was never finished, for the designer discovered that the enormous stone had several flaws at the extreme end.

Modern engineers marvel that the Egyptians were able to stand these shafts on end without breaking them. They did so by using ramps. Also, they understood practical higher mathematics. Records have been discovered which indicate they could work practical problems with two unknown quantities.

The top portion of each obelisk was covered with gold. Thus, when the sun shown on it, it glittered like a flame.

After Hatshepsut died in 1496 B.C., her nephew Thutmose III whom she had dominated, began to rule with complete authority. He defaced many of his aunt's monuments. On some, he replaced her name with that of his own, or that of his father or grandfather. The obelisks were a problem. Since it would be inexpedient to topple them, he did the next best thing. He built other nearby structures in order to lessen their importance.

The buildings, monuments, obelisks, murals, temples, palaces, and banqueting halls cost vast sums of money. Where did they get it? From tribute!

Egypt's many festivals kept the banquet halls busy. The most joyous festival was that known as "the beginning of eternity and the end of everlasting time." That one was in honor of the New Year. Each season had a festival; and there was a festival in honor of the "overflowing Nile" and so on.

During the New Year's festival, lights were burned on the West Bank, and small boats were pointed toward the banqueting halls on the other side. This was so that the dead pharaohs buried on the west side of the Nile might also enjoy the celebration. At each banquet there was an abundance of flowers. There were flowers on the tables, in elaborate vases, and even on the floor. Also, there were large tables on which were piled gifts for the gods.

Egyptians used knives and spoons, but at this time forks had not been invented and so it was quite proper to use one's fingers. As the people gorged, orchestras played, and small naked girls danced. One elaborate course followed another; and as the guests feasted they washed the food down with wine and huge flagons of beer.

The drinking continued hour after hour. When it flagged, waiters brought small mummies into the hall. The implication was, "You will be a mummy after a while, and so enjoy yourself while you can." The revelers never suffered from bad conscience. This is because they were convinced that the gods enjoyed watching their drunken orgies. A rich woman of Thebes who preceded her husband in death, arranged for the following sign to be mounted within her tomb:

> Be drunken, enjoy the love of women, make
> holiday. Follow thy desire by night and day.

Moses witnessed all of these things. He also saw the vast amounts of gold that were fashioned into coffins, statues, jewelry. But after he had spoken to the Lord at the Burning Bush in Midian, he lost all desire—if he ever had any—for material wealth and the pleasures of Egypt. From that moment on he was an extremely happy man even though he constantly faced overwhelming difficulty. There is no record that he ever longed to return to the fleshpots of Egypt.

Chapter 19

Babylon: City of Power

Other than Jerusalem, Babylon influenced Jewish life more than any other city. While there in exile, the Jews learned to be businessmen, to follow the professions—and to take advantage of compound interest!

The name Babylon comes from the Accadian word *Babilu*. Ironically, that name means "Gate of God."

Altogether, Babylon is mentioned in the Bible almost three hundred times. The first mention is in II Kings 17:24, when the Assyrians brought people from Babylon and other places to repopulate Samaria when the people of Israel were taken captive. The last mention is a symbolic reference in Revelation 18 where it is used to depict evil. Between these extremes, Jeremiah uttered a scorching prophecy that has been fulfilled.

Even while Nebuchadnezzar was preparing to besiege Jerusalem, Jeremiah strode around the soon-to-be-crushed city and prophesied:

> And Babylon shall become heaps, a dwelling place for dragons, an astonishment, and an hissing, without an inhabitant (Jeremiah 51:37).

As Jeremiah spoke, many of his listeners must have had strange looks on their faces, for at the time, Babylon was the largest, strongest, richest, and most magnificent city on earth. It was protected by a large army, adequate water supplies, excellent scientific knowledge—and several formidable walls. One wall was so thick there was room on its top for a four-horse chariot to pass another—and even to turn around. Moreover, its fifty gates were made of heavy bronze.

The statement that someday Babylon would be no more was considered as impossible as the statement that one plus three equals thirteen. Nonetheless, Jeremiah's prophecy came to pass. But Jeremiah was not the only prophet who envisioned what would happen to the great city of the Euphrates. Isaiah wrote: "And Babylon, the glory of kingdoms, the beauty of the Chaldees' excellency, shall be as when God overthrew Sodom and Gomorrah. It shall never be inhabited, neither shall it be dwelt in from generation to generation: neither shall the Arabian pitch tent there; neither shall the shepherds make their fold there. But wild beasts of the desert shall lie there; and their houses shall be full of doleful creatures; and owls shall dwell there, and satyrs shall dance there. And the wild beasts of the islands shall cry in their desolate houses, and dragons in their pleasant palaces: and her time is near to come, and her days shall not be prolonged" (13:19-22).

Today, the great Babylon is nothing but a heap of ruins just as Isaiah and Jeremiah had predicted. Its only inhabitants are owls, jackals, and other hateful animals. The ruins are near the modern city of al-Hillah, about 55 miles south of Baghdad in central Iraq. The city's former great walls, wide avenues, temples, palaces, homes, are no more. Many of the bricks have inscribed on them in cuneiform the names of former rulers. But the only good these bricks accomplish at this time is to underline to visitors that this was once the greatest and most feared city in the world—that it was here that Daniel survived the den of lions, and Shadrach, Meshach, and Abednego survived one of its fiery furnaces.

Dim whiffs from ancient writings indicate that Babylon had obscure beginnings as far back as the third millennium B.C.

But it did not become a city to be reckoned with until about the twenty-third century B.C. In that long, long ago, walls began to be laid. Then Hammurabi (1792-1750) strode onto the scene. He conquered the surrounding city-states, made Babylon his capital, and announced that Marduk was the god of Babylon and that in solemn assembly the other gods had elected Marduk as their leader.Some researchers speculate that this indicates the beginnings of henotheism (one god supreme among many) among Gentiles. A poem from this period relates the decision made by the gods:

> Your destiny is unrivalled, your utterance is Anu. O Marduk! You are the honored one among the great gods . . . We have given you kingship over everything. (Quoted from *The Greatness That Was Babylon*.)

Marduk was married to *Sarpanitum*—"The shining one." (In this, he was like other gods.) He had at least fifty separate names, including *Bel* which is mentioned in Isaiah 46:1.

This chapter, however, is not a history of Babylon. Rather it is about what Babylon was like during the period in which the Jews were there in exile and later when they were freed by the decree of Cyrus.

Following the death of Ashurbanipal, a Chaldean leader, Nabopolassar founded the Neo-Babylonian Empire and made Babylon his capital in 626 B.C. Nabopolassar was followed by his son Nebuchadnezzar—technically Nebuchadnezzar II.

The moment the youthful Nebuchadnezzar came to power in 605, he began to enlarge, beautify, and fortify Babylon. Like other rulers in this period, he financed much of this work with funds he received from tribute paid by nations he dominated. And since tribute was being paid to him by Judah at this time, some of their money must have gone into building projects.

Herodotus was impressed by the Babylon he saw. (He probably visited the city around 450 B.C. This was about two centuries after the times of Nebuchadnezzar.) He wrote: "The city stands on a broad plain, and is an exact square, a hundred and twenty furlongs [a little over 5 miles] in length each way . . . While such is its size, in magnificence there is no other city that approaches to it. . . .

"The city is divided into two portions by the river which runs through the midst of it. This river is the Euphrates, a broad, deep, swift stream . . . The houses are mostly three and four stories high; the streets run in straight lines. . . .

"The outer wall is the main defence of the city . . . In the middle of the precinct there was a tower of solid masonry, a furlong [a furlong is 220 yards] in length and breadth, upon which was raised a second tower, and on that a third, and so on up to eight. The ascent to the top is on the outside . . . On the topmost tower there is a spacious temple, and inside the temple stands a couch of unusual size, richly adorned with a golden table by its side. There is no statue of any kind set up in the place, nor is the chamber occupied of nights by anyone but a single native woman. . .

"They also declare—but I for my part do not credit it—that the god comes down in person into this chamber, and sleeps upon the couch." (Some writers think this was the Tower of Babel.)

A main accomplishment of Nebuchadnezzar was that of the construction of the Ishtar Gate. This forty-foot-high entrance stood between two high towers. The surrounding area was ornamented with glazed bricks and five hundred and seventy-five bulls and dragons worked into the walls. The dragons were especially sacred to Marduk. This elaborate gate opened into Procession Street—the Babylonian equivalent of the Champs Elysees in Paris.

All of the streets in Babylon were named after one of their gods. On the left bank there was Marduk Street, Zababa Street, and so on. These streets crossed the one named after the moon god. Adad Street was a main artery on the right bank. It was intersected by Shamash named after the sun god.

Nebuchadnezzar was extremely proud of this building program. Daniel heard him boast about it, and quoted him as saying: "Is not this great Babylon, that I have built for the house of the kingdom by the might of my power, and for the honor of my majesty?" (Daniel 4:30).

How did people live in this, the most famous city in the contemporary world? In order to know that, we'll take a brief look at various aspects of their society.

Slavery. Like in Rome during New Testament times, most of the hard work was done by slaves. Many of the slaves were prisoners of war. Others were native Babylonians, for it was quite possible for a father to sell his wife and children into slavery. A bill of sale from the times of Nebuchadnezzar has survived. The document reads:

> The children of Zakir, son of X . . . , have of their free will sold to the son of Y . . . their slave Nana-dirat and the child which she is suckling, at the agreed price of 19 shekels of silver. The sellers will guarantee the purchaser against her flight or a counter claim, or if she is found to be royal property or free (*Everyday Life in Babylon and Assyria*).

Like every nation in history, Babylonia suffered from inflation. This can be noted in the price of slaves. During the reign of Nebuchadnezzar the price averaged 40 shekels; under Nabonidus it went up to 50 shekels; and under Cyrus it soared to 60 shekels.

The value of a shekel can be estimated by the amount of wages paid. Two temple guards were paid 34 shekels for twelve days of duty. Assuming these wages were divided equally among them, each earned a little less than a shekel and a half a day. That would mean that in the days of Cyrus, a slave could be purchased for less than 43 days of work.

Slaves who might escape were branded. Many had tags bearing their owner's name chained around their necks. Some masters had their slaves' heads shaved so as to make them conspicuous. A caricature of the life of a slave is indicated in a piece of contemporary satire:

> "Slave, make yourself agreeable."
> "Yes, sir, yes."
> "Fetch water for my hands straightaway and give it
> to me,
> So that I may make a sacrifice to my god. . . ."

The master then comments: "You can train him so that he keeps trotting behind you like a dog."

Many masters had children by their slaves; and these children were frequently sold by the masters on the slave market.

Housing. Stone and trees were extremely scarce in Babylonia. This means that the average house was made of sun-dried brick which had been laced with straw. Burned bricks were, of course, far more permanent than those dried in the sun. But fuel in Mesopotamia was exceedingly scarce. A typical house had a beaten-earth floor, was windowless, and was roofed with palm limbs over which palm leaves were laid in thick piles.

The outside walls were frequently whitewashed.

Garbage was thrown out onto the street where it was either devoured by dogs or eventually dried in the hot sun and was gradually pulverized by the feet of those who passed by.

Furniture consisted of mats for beds, a low table or two, and perhaps a cupboard. Cooking was done over a charcoal brazier. Artificial lighting was by candle or flat saucer-lamps in which a wick had been placed. These lamps were fueled by "stone-oil"—that is, unrefined crude oil.

There is some evidence that sulphur matches were in use. Normally, however, a fire was started by striking flint against iron.

Business. Werner Keller in his book *The Bible as History*, tells about a typical business founded by exiled Jews. This business, Murashu and Sons, dealt in many services: loans, real estate, insurance, jewelry, international banking.

"One day three jewelers called on Murashu and Sons." A document from the business transaction states: "Elil-Aha-Idinna and Belsunu and Hatin said to Elil-Nadin-Sum, son of Murashu: 'In the case of this emerald ring, we give a twenty years' guarantee that the stone will not fall out of the gold. If the emerald falls out of the ring before the expiry of twenty years, Elil-Aha-Idinna, Belsanu and Hatin undertake to pay damages to Elil-Nadin-Sum amounting to 10 Minas of silver.' "

The signatures of seven people are on the document, and since the jewelers were illiterate, they agreed to the contract by pressing their fingernails into the moist clay tablet.

Interest was 20 percent!

Medicine. Many illnesses in Babylonia were declared to be caused by the breaking of a taboo, or the offending of a god. For example:

> If the door of someone's house, where the sick man is lying, cries out [creaks] like a lion, he has eaten the taboo of his god; he will drag out and then die.
>
> If a sick man keeps crying out 'My skull! My skull!' [it] is the hand of a god.
>
> If he grinds his teeth, and his hands and feet shake, it is the hand of the god Sin; he will die.
>
> If his neck throbs and his head keeps falling, and his hands and feet keep swelling up and he rubs

[them] against the ground; the demon Handmaid of Lilu has seized him.

Numerous medicines were prescribed. The following are typical:

If pain seizes on a man, you shall put . . . gum of Aleppo pine, gum of galbanum and tumeric on the fire and shall fumigate his nostril [therewith]; you shall fill your mouth with oil and shall blow into his nostrils, and he will recover.

If a man's stomach is hot, and will not accept food or drink, you shall take the seed of tamarisk, and mix [it] with honey and curd. He shall eat and recover.

(From ancient texts used in Babylon. Quoted from *The Greatness That Was Babylon*.)

Religion. A contemporary inscription reveals that Babylon was a city of temples, shrines, and places of worship. "There are altogether in Babylon fifty-three temples of the great gods, fifty-five shrines dedicated to Marduk, three hundred shrines belonging to earth divinities, one hundred and eighty altars to the goddess Ishtar, one hundred and eighty to the gods Nergal and Adad, and twelve others to various deities."

The temple built for Marduk was by far the largest. The remains that have been so far excavated indicate that it was 470 feet long—a mere fifty feet shorter than St. Paul's in London! The temple was served by many priests. Still, the king was the high priest; and it was he who took charge on top occasions. He even officiated at many of the animal sacrifices—even though a priest might have to instruct him as to each move he should make.

This huge temple was destroyed several times; but, on each occasion, it was repaired or rebuilt.

A ziggurat, similar to the one at Ur, stood near the temple. It was at the pinnacle of this huge pyramid-shaped mound that their most sacred ceremonies were enacted.

Although Marduk was considered supreme, other gods also were greatly honored. Herodotus wrote about another place of worship. "Below, in the same precinct, there is a second temple, in which is a sitting figure of Jupiter, all of gold. Before the figure stands a large golden table, and the throne whereon it sits, and the base on which the throne is placed, are likewise of gold. The Chaldaeans told me that all the gold together was eight hundred talents' weight [twenty-five tons]. Outside the temple are two altars, one of solid gold, on which it is only lawful to offer sucklings; the other a common altar, but of great size on which the full-grown animals are sacrificed. It is also on the great altar that the Chaldaeans burn frankincense, which is offered to the amount of a thousand talents' weight, every year, at the festival of the god. In the time of Cyrus there was likewise in this temple a figure of a man, twelve cubits high, entirely of solid gold. I myself did not see this figure. . ." (Herodotus, Book I). (The above figures seem utterly incredible. Herodotus often exaggerated. Nonetheless, archaeology has proved that many of his extravagant statements were at least nearly correct!)

Temple prostitution was a part of Babylonian worship. Fathers who bequeathed their daughters to this task were honored. Temple prostitutes were forbidden by law to enter public eating places. Those who became pregnant were forced to have abortions. A "sacred" prostitute was required to remain childless and to serve for thirty years. All temple priestesses, however, were not prostitutes.

Morals. Although a native of Greece where public morals were low, Herodotus was shocked by what he saw in Babylon. He wrote: "The Babylonians have one most shameful custom. Every woman born in the country must once in her life go and sit down in the precinct of Venus, and there consort with a stranger . . . A woman who has taken her seat is not allowed to return home till one of the strangers throws a silver coin in her lap, and takes her with him beyond the holy ground. When he throws the coin he says these words, 'The goddess Mylitta prosper thee.' Venus is called Mylitta by the Assyrians. The silver coin may be of any size; it cannot be refused, for that is forbidden by law, since once thrown it is sacred. The woman goes with the first man who throws money and rejects no one. When she has gone with him, and so satisfied the goddess, she returns home, and from that time forth no gift however great will prevail with her" (Herodotus, Book I).

Having had Jewish exiles in the city for seventy years, the Babylonians knew all about the prophecies of Isaiah and Jeremiah that predicted their destruction. But they laughed at those prophecies, just as Belshazzar had laughed prior to when the hand wrote upon the wall during the great feast. It was just impossible to imagine that their city could be destroyed. After all, they were a most distinguished nation. They were first in mathematics—our sixty minute hour, sixty second minute, and three hundred and sixty degree circle go back to them. Also, they were rich, had lots of religion, were first in science, and first in literature—and their medicine was famous everywhere.

Nonetheless, God had spoken!

Herodotus wrote about one of Babylon's rebellions against the Persians. "At last when the time came for rebelling openly they [the Babylonians] did as follows: having first set apart their mothers, each man chose besides out of his whole household one woman, whomsoever he pleased; these alone were allowed to live, while all the rest were brought to one place and strangled. The women chosen were kept to make bread for the men; while the others were strangled that they might not consume the stores.

"When tidings reached Darius of what had happened, he drew together all his power, and began to war by marching straight on Babylon, and laying siege to the place. The Babylonians . . . cared not a whit for his siege. Mounting upon the battlements that crowned their walls, they insulted and jeered at Darius and his mighty host. One even shouted to them and said, 'Why sit ye there, Persians? why do ye not go back to your homes? Till mules foal ye will not take our city.' This was said by a Babylonian who thought a mule would never foal" (Herodotus, Book III).

Months went by during which the Babylonians continued to hold out and to jeer at Darius. But finally Darius was successful. Then, according to Herodotus, "he chose out near three thousand of the leading citizens, and caused them to be crucified, while he allowed the remainder to occupy the city..." (Herodotus, Book III).

Eventually Babylon continued on in a semi-healthy state. Then it was conquered by Alexander the Great in 331 B.C. After Alexander's death in 323, the city came under the control of Seleucus Nicator. This new ruler built a new capital, Seleucia, on the banks of the Tigris and transported great quantities of building materials from Babylon to the new city. From that point, Babylon continued in its rapid decline.

The city of Babylon is no more.

The prophecies of Isaiah and Jeremiah were fulfilled.

Chapter 20

Sodom: City of Sin

Few cities have been forgotten as completely and yet remembered as completely as Sodom and its neighboring city Gomorrah. Sodom is mentioned 49 times in 15 books of the Bible. Moreover, its character smudged the word sodomite into being; and that horror-laced word is mentioned five times in three additional Biblical books.

Today, no city on earth is named Sodom!

The story of Sodom begins in Genesis 10:19 where we are informed that the "border of the Canaanites ran from Sidon toward Gerar and down to Gaza; then to Sodom and Gomorrah." This brief geographical description enables us to understand a major problem that had arisen between Abraham and his nephew Lot.

> And Abram was very rich in cattle, in silver, and in gold . . . And Lot also, which went with Abram, had flocks, and herds, and tents. And the land was not able to bear them, that they might dwell together . . . And there was a strife between the herdmen of Abram's cattle and the herdmen of Lot's cattle: and the Canaanite and the Perizzite dwelled then in the land (Genesis 13:2,5-7).

Following this excitement, the plot of Abraham's life made

an unusual twist. In a vision, the Lord assured him that his descendants would be as numerous as the stars. Later, God made a covenant with Abraham: "Unto thy seed have I given this land, from the river of Egypt [the Nile] unto the great river, the river Euphrates" (Genesis 15:18).

Later, after the Lord had instructed Abraham as to the rite of circumcision, three men—actually they were angels—appeared at his tent. One of them assured him that his wife Sarah would have a son, and two of them let him know that God was sending them to Sodom to see whether or not it should be destroyed. It was at this point that Abraham had his famous conversation with the Lord.

Said Abraham: "Peradventure there be fifty righteous within the city: wilt thou also destroy and not spare the place for the fifty righteous that are therein?" (Genesis 18:24). When the Lord agreed that He would spare the city if He found within it fifty righteous, Abraham kept lowering his figure, until the Lord agreed that He would not destroy it for the sake of even ten. The conversation over, we read that two angels arrived at Sodom and stopped at the home of Lot.

> And there came two angels to Sodom at even;
> and Lot sat in the gate of Sodom: and Lot seeing
> them rose up to meet them; and he bowed himself
> with his face toward the ground (Genesis 19:1).

This passage goes on to explain how Lot fed them and insisted that they spend the night with him. Being angels, the two were unusually handsome "men." Soon the word about their appearance spread in the city. A spokesman for the crowd of lustful men that soon gathered, said: "Where are the men which came in to thee this night? bring them out unto us, that we may know them" (vs. 5). The words *know them* mean: be sexually intimate with them. That passage in the *New English Bible* reads: "Bring them out," they shouted, "so that we can have intercourse with them." Instead of the word *intercourse*, the *Living Bible* uses the sinister term "rape."

179

Josephus added even more color to the scene: "Now when the Sodomites saw the young men to be of beautiful countenances . . . they resolved themselves to enjoy these beautiful boys by force and violence" (*Antiquities of the Jews*, Chapter XI, part 4).

Utterly horrified by the frank demands of the men, Lot had a suggestion: "Behold now, I have two daughters which have not known man; let me, I pray you, bring them out unto you, and do ye to them as is good in your eyes: only unto these men do nothing . . ." (vs. 8). It was a terrible suggestion, but Lot was desperate.

Again, Josephus adds a dimension: "And when Lot exhorted them to sobriety . . . but to have regard to their lodging in his house; and promised that if their inclinations could not be governed, he would expose his daughters to their lust . . . neither were they made ashamed" (*Antiquities of the Jews*, Chapter XI, part 4).

A tussle ensued when Lot refused to let the men in; and, as they pushed at the door, they threatened Lot. "Stand back!" they shouted. Then, after repeating this warning, the ninth verse records that one of them said, "This . . . fellow came in to sojourn, and he will needs be a judge: now will we deal worse with thee, than with them. And they pressed sore upon . . . Lot, and came near to break the door."

The drama continues in verses ten and eleven. "But the men [angels] put forth their hand, and pulled Lot into the house to them, and shut to the door. And they [the angels] smote the men that were at the door of the house with blindness, both small and great: so that they wearied themselves to find the door."

The visiting angels then warned Lot to take his family and flee the city. After they escaped to Zoar, "the Lord rained upon Sodom and upon Gomorrah brimstone and fire from the Lord out of heaven" (vs. 24).

The smoke must have been dense, for we read, "And Abraham gat up early in the morning . . . and he looked toward

Sodom and Gomorrah, and toward all the land of the plain, and beheld, and, lo, the smoke of the country went up as the smoke of a furnace" (vss. 27-28).

What did the Lord use to accomplish this judgment? There was crude oil near the surface in this area and scientists believe that there were numerous natural gas leaks. That there was petroleum in the vicinity is indicated in Genesis 14:10. "And the vale of Siddim was full of slimepits. . . ." *The New English Bible* renders *slimepits* "bitumen pits" and the *Living Bible* renders the words "asphalt pits."

It is commonly known that this Dead Sea area which reaches a depth of 1,291 feet below sea level is the lowest place in the world and that it is rich in flammable deposits. In describing the Dead Sea area, Josephus wrote: "The nature of the lake Asphalitis [Dead Sea] is . . . worth describing . . . When Vespasian went to see it, he commanded that some who could not swim should have their hands tied behind them, and be thrown into the deep, when it so happened that they all swam as if a wind had forced them upwards." He then wrote about the "black clods of bitumen." "This bitumen is not only useful for the caulking of ships, but for the cure of men's bodies; accordingly it is mixed in a great many medicines" (*Of the War*, Book IV, Chapter VIII, section 4).

Josephus also explained how Sodom and Gomorrah were set on fire. "God then cast a thunderbolt upon the city and set it on fire . . . and laid waste the country with the burning" (*Antiquities*, Chapter XI, Book 1, part 4).

Today, the actual city of Sodom is no more. Even traces have not been found. It is suspected that the old ruins are now covered by the southern end of the Dead Sea. Sodom's memory, however, still lingers. It was mentioned in the New Testament ten times—first in Matthew 10:15, and finally in Revelation 11:8. Of Sodom, Jesus said, "And thou, Capernaum, which art exalted unto heaven, shalt be brought down to hell: for if the mighty works, which have been done in thee, had been done in Sodom, it would have remained until this day"

SODOM

(Matthew 11:23).

During the last week of August, A.D. 79, the inhabitants of Pompeii noticed that a tall spume was rising from Vesuvius less than a mile away and was getting higher and blacker by the minute. But even though the volcano had erupted many times before and had been ominously growling since 63, few paid any attention. The citizens were used to disasters. At the time, they were rebuilding from the devastating earthquake of 62.

An unknown Christian or Jew, however, felt disaster was near. Obeying an impulse he scribbled on a wall of the city: "Sodoma Gomorra."

On August 24 Pompeii was no more!

Chapter 21

Bethel: City of Memories

Unlike Sodom and Gomorrah, the name *Bethel* has not disappeared, nor does it have a negative connotation. Indeed, it's a favorite name—especially in the United States.

Even though the word Bethel never appears in the New Testament, there are eighteen cities in the United States that derive their names from Bethel. In addition, that name is on colleges, churches, camps, boats—and many streets. Curiously, there are only ten *Bethanies* in both the United States and Canada. Moreover, Bethany was the hometown of Mary, Martha, and Lazarus. Also, Bethany was the city where Jesus raised Lazarus from the dead

Why is Bethany which means "house of poverty" less popular than Bethel which means "house of God"? No one knows. But there are some surface reasons why a farmer should not even name his barn Bethel! Let's look at some of those reasons.

1. The first reason is quite insignificant. Still, it's a reason. In the long, long ago Bethel started out as a Canaanite city where the people worshiped a false El—a heathen god.

2. When, after Solomon's death in 931, Jeroboam I split the kingdom by separating the ten tribes into the Northern Kingdom, he made Bethel his sanctuary, and erected golden calves there even though he claimed to be a follower of

Jehovah. Thus, Bethel became the sanctuary of a new cult. This Canaanite cult became entrenched in Bethel and, in time, added Asherah (Lady of the Sea) and wife of El to the list of their gods.

3. Bethel is remembered for the gang of young hoodlums who taunted Elisha, "Go up, thou bald head; go up, thou bald head." The prophet's response was rather severe. Elisha "cursed them in the name of the Lord. And there came forth two she bears out of the wood, and tare forty and two children of them" (II Kings 2:23-24).

4. Before the Israelite invasion of Canaan, Bethel was a beautiful city with excellent streets and buildings. But the new Bethel that replaced the one burned by Joshua was a very inadequate city filled with second-class structures. It was a despised little town.

5. Bethel was destroyed and rebuilt at least four times between 1200 and 1000 B.C. Sometimes the city was ruled by Ephraim and at other times by Benjamin. It was not a stable city.

6. The prophets denounced it. Hosea called it *Bethaven*— House of Naught (Hosea 4:15). Amos was sarcastic. Said he, "Come to Bethel, and transgress" (Amos 4:4). And Jeremiah lamented, "The house of Israel was ashamed of Bethel" (48:13).

With all of this negative evidence, why should a church or a city be named Bethel? Because many of these negative defects became transformed into positive virtues! Here are some of them.

1. Abraham built an altar at Bethel. "And he removed from thence unto a mountain on the east of Beth-el, and pitched his tent . . . and there he builded an altar unto the Lord" (Genesis 12:8).

2. Bethel was the place where Jacob had his vision of a ladder ascending up to heaven. Upon awakening, he was so

deeply moved, he exclaimed, "Surely the Lord is in this place; and I knew it not" (Genesis 28:16). Next we are told, "And Jacob rose up early in the morning, and took the stone that he had put for his pillows, and set it up for a pillar, and poured oil on the top of it. And he called the name of that place Beth-el: but the name of that city was called Luz at the first" (vss. 18-19). (Luz means almond tree.)

3. Bethel was where Jacob's name was changed. "And God said unto him, Thy name is Jacob: thy name shall not be called any more Jacob, but Israel shall be thy name: and he called his name Israel" (Genesis 35:10).

4. The Abrahamic covenant was renewed with Jacob, now Israel, at Bethel. "And God said unto him, I am God Almighty: be fruitful and multiply; a nation and a company of nations shall be of thee, and kings shall come out of thy loins" (vs. 11).

5. The Ark of the Covenant was located at Bethel for a time (Judges 20:27-28).

6. A school for the prophets was located at Bethel. "So they [Elijah and Elisha] went down to Beth-el and the sons of the prophets that were at Beth-el came forth. . ." (II Kings 2:2-3).

7. An amazing prophecy was fulfilled at Bethel. The first act in this scene took place about the year 930 B.C. Jeroboam was there burning incense on the new Canaanitish altar he had constructed when a prophet appeared. Facing the altar, this unnamed man of God had a solemn statement. "O altar, altar, thus saith the Lord; Behold, a child shall be born unto the house of David, Josiah by name; and upon thee shall he offer the priests of the high places that burn incense upon thee, and men's bones shall be burnt upon thee. And he gave a sign the same day, saying, This is the sign which the Lord hath spoken; Behold, the altar shall be rent, and the ashes that are upon it shall be poured out" (I Kings 13:2-3).

The second act began in 620—over three centuries later. "And he [Josiah] brake in pieces the images, and cut down the groves, and filled their places with the bones of men. Moreover the altar that was at Beth-el, and the high place which Jeroboam the son of Nebat, who made Israel to sin, had made, both that altar and the high place he brake down, and burned the high place, and stamped it small to powder, and burned the grove. And as Josiah turned himself, he spied the sepulchres, that were there in the mount, and sent, and took the bones out of the sepulchres, and burned them upon the altar, and polluted it, according to the word of the Lord which the man of God proclaimed" (II Kings 23:14-16).

This drama has yet a third act. While Josiah was busy burning the bones of the Canaanitish priests, he noticed an unusual sepulchre. When he inquired what it was "the men of the city told him, It is the sepulchre of the man of God which came from Judah, and proclaimed these things that thou has done against the altar of Beth-el" (vs. 17).

Josiah then gave an order: "Let him alone; let no man move his bones. So they let his bones alone" (vs. 18).

Considering these supernatural events, it is easy to see the reason for the popularity of the name Bethel in modern times. It was a place where new names were given, old wrongs righted, men inspired, prophets taught.

It had also witnessed the sternness of God's laws!

Bethel had an excellent water supply. This is indicated by the numbers of those who returned there after the Exile. Ezra listed 223 (Ezra 2:28). Nehemiah noted 123 (Nehemiah 7:32). Why the difference? Bethel is a mere twelve miles north of Jerusalem. Could it be that a number of Bethel residents moved to Jerusalem in order to help Nehemiah rebuild the walls? His task was great and he needed all the help he could procure.

Excavations at Bethel have underlined that it was burned by the invading Israelites during the Bronze Age.

Chapter 22

Jericho:
Symbol of the Impossible

No Bible-loving tourist would choose to miss Jericho!

Only seventeen miles northeast of Jerusalem as the crow flies, Jericho overflows with interest. On the way, as the bus moves down the winding road, one passes the legendary inn where the Good Samaritan lodged, the victim of the thieves; and, in palm-filled Jericho, one can see Elisha's Fount which was "healed" by the prophet. Moreover, Jericho sings with memories: Zacchaeus, blind men, the crowds that thronged Jesus.

Ah, but those sites and memories are in New Testament Jericho. This chapter is about Old Testament Jericho!

Most cities tumbled by earthquakes or otherwise destroyed rebuild on the same location. Many use the remains of the same foundations. But not Jericho! The sites of its various moves are listed by archaeologists as City A, City B, and so on. British archaeologist John Garstang who labored on the Jericho project from 1930 to 1936 is convinced that the Old Testament Jericho destroyed by Joshua was City D.

When excavators started swinging their picks at Tell es-Sultan—City D—in 1907, Professor Ernst Sellin and Professor Karl Watzinger were soon able to grab headlines around the world. This is because they discovered that Old

Jericho was a masterpiece of fortifications. There were two parallel walls that encircled the city. The outer wall was from twenty-five to thirty feet high and about six feet thick. The inside wall, about twelve feet away, was approximately twelve feet thick.

After a thorough examination, Garstang widened eyes by writing: "The space between the two walls is filled with fragments and rubble. There are clear traces of a tremendous fire, compact masses of blackened bricks, cracked stones, charred wood, and ashes. Along the walls the houses have been burned to the ground and their roofs have crashed on top of them."

This report widened smiles on the faces of Christians, for the Book of Joshua states: ". . . and the people shouted with a great shout [and] the wall fell down flat . . . And they burnt the city with fire, and all that was therein" (Joshua 6:20-24).

But was this the Jericho Joshua faced? Following her work which began in Jericho in 1952, Kathleen Kenyon became doubtful. She even suggested that the Jericho of Joshua's day was "little more than a fort."

Much of the controversy over Old Testament Jericho revolves around the dating of the Exodus. Gleason L. Archer has made some illuminating remarks about this in his excellent book *Encyclopedia of Bible Difficulties*. Disputing the later suggested date of the Exodus—1250 B.C.—he wrote: ". . . The testimony of the cemetery connected with City IV (D) at Tell es-Sultan . . . is quite conclusive in favor of a date around 1400 B.C. which is in complete conformity with a 1446 date of the Exodus itself. After several years of thorough archaeological investigation, John Garstang discovered that of the many scarabs found in the graves of this cemetery, not a single one dates from a period later than Amenhotep III of Egypt (1412-1376 B.C.)."

But instead of pausing to study the new battle of Jericho where pots and jewelry and scarabs are compared, let's go back to the battle fought by Joshua. (For a discussion of the dates of the Exodus, see chapter 6 of this book.)

Since the battle of Jericho was the first battle fought after the Israelites had crossed the Jordan, the writers of the Book of Joshua devoted an entire chapter to that battle. This is significant—and helpful, for it outlines how God overcomes impossibilities in seemingly impossible ways.

Joshua's task of leadership after the death of Moses was formidable. The Israelites had grumbled about Moses even though he understood all the wisdom of Egypt and could have wasted his life in self-indulgence. He, Joshua, was not the "son of pharaoh's daughter." How could he get them to follow him? Joshua need not have worried, for the Lord made a way by providing an obstacle—the swollen Jordan river!

As Joshua viewed the river, he must have wondered why the Lord had not arranged it so that they would have either arrived at this place a few months earlier or a few months later. Had the Lord done that, the river would have been so low even the women could have waded across!

Being a prudent man, Joshua sent two unnamed spies across the Jordan to investigate Jericho. These men lodged with the harlot Rahab whose house was on the wall. This house was quite strategic, for her customers tended to have loose tongues, and from the high position they had an excellent view of the city, and the surrounding country.

From this public woman the spies learned three important things. (1) She said, "For we have heard how the Lord dried up . . . the Red sea for you." (2) Then she continued, "[And we have learned] what ye did unto the two kings of the Amorites, that were on the other side Jordan, Sihon and Og, whom ye utterly destroyed." (3) Her conclusion was, "And as soon as we heard these things, our hearts did melt. . ." (Joshua 2:10-11).

All of this was excellent news for the spies. Then, after she had hidden them, and thus saved their lives, she requested a favor of them. That favor was that they spare both her life and those of her relatives. She then used a crimson cord to help them escape through a window. In answer to Rahab's request for mercy, the spies said: "Behold, when we come into the land, thou shalt bind this line of scarlet thread in the window which thou didst let us down by: and thou shalt bring thy father, and thy mother, and thy brethren, and all thy father's household home unto thee" (vs. 18).

Joshua was delighted with this report. But an utter impossibility stretched out in front of him. That impossibility was the river Jordan! There were no boats nor bridges. And since his followers had been in the wilderness for the last forty years, few, if any, knew how to swim. But Joshua had received a command from the Lord; and, as impossible of accomplishment as it seemed, he was prepared to obey. His first task was to relay the Lord's instructions to the people.

Joshua's instructions were simple. The priests were to carry the Ark of the Covenant to the Jordan, enter the riverbed, stop in its midst, and the people were to pass by.

As the people listened, eyes must have questioned. Did some of them have long thoughts? If so, it is not recorded that there were any negative comments!

Here's what happened:

> And as they that bare the ark were come unto Jordan, and the feet of the priests that bare the ark were dipped in the brim of the water . . . the waters which came down from above stood and rose up upon an heap . . . and those that came down toward the sea of the plain, even the salt sea, failed, and were cut off: and the people passed over right against Jericho . . . and all the Israelites passed over on dry ground, until all the people were passed clean over Jordan (Joshua 3:15-17).

History has recorded several occasions when the Jordan river stopped flowing and people were enabled to cross on dry land. But on this occasion it stopped at the right place

190

and the right time.

Two great things were accomplished that day. The children of Israel, many tens of thousands of them, crossed over onto the other side of Jordan, and the leadership of Joshua was confirmed. As the multitude waited for the last straggler to cross, many must have wondered what their leader would do next.

Joshua's next announcement was sensational.

"During the last forty years no one has been circumcised," said Joshua. "This means that all males must be circumcised at once."

"But the battle of Jericho is just ahead!" exclaimed a broad-shouldered man.

"That doesn't make any difference! Jehovah must be obeyed; and Jehovah said to me 'Make thee sharp knives, and circumcise again the children of Israel' " (Joshua 5:2).

There were a few groans. Joshua ignored them. "We will use flint knives," he explained. "It will be painful. But God must be obeyed."

(The reason for this announcement is explained in the fifth verse: "Now all the people that came out [of Egypt] were circumcised: but all the people that were born in the wilderness by the way as they came forth out of Egypt, them they had not circumcised.")

The fact, however, that this announcement was made just prior to a major battle seems incredible. It would be as if the moment after D day the Allied generals had announced: "Now before we head for Paris all of those who have not been circumcised will have to be circumcised. Then, after they've recovered we'll start across France."

Nonetheless, Joshua was merely obeying the Lord! Verse nine explains the Lord's reasoning: "And the Lord said unto Joshua, This day have I rolled away the reproach of Egypt from off you."

After the men had recovered at Gilgal, they celebrated the

passover on the fourteenth. The Israelites were then ready to take Jericho. Ah, but the Lord wasn't! Verse thirteen explains what happened: "And it came to pass, when Joshua was by Jericho, that he lifted up his eyes and looked, and, behold, there stood a man over against him with his sword drawn in his hand: and Joshua went unto him, and said unto him, Art thou for us, or for our adversaries? And he said, Nay; but as captain of the host of the Lord am I now come. And Joshua fell on his face to the earth, and did worship, and said unto him, What saith my lord unto his servant?

"And the captain of the Lord's host said unto Joshua, Loose thy shoe from off thy foot; for the place whereon thou standest is holy. And Joshua did so" (Joshua 5:13-15).

Joshua had, of course, spoken to the Lord Jesus Christ in what theologians term a theophany. Obviously the Lord had appeared to him in this way just as He had appeared to Moses at the Burning Bush in order to give him courage and assurance.

The instructions the Lord gave Joshua in order to take Jericho were even stranger than those He had given him in order to enable the children of Israel to cross the Jordan. Had Joshua not just had his recent experience with the Lord, he might have laughed. Those instructions are recorded in Joshua 6:3-5.

> And ye shall compass the city, all ye men of war, and go round about the city once. Thus shalt thou do six days. And seven priests shall bear before the ark seven trumpets of rams' horns: and the seventh day ye shall compass the city seven times, and the priests shall blow with the trumpets. And it shall come to pass, that when they make a long blast with the ram's horn, and when ye hear the sound of the trumpet, all the people shall shout with a great shout; and the wall of the city shall fall down flat, and the people shall ascend up every man straight

before him.

Joshua relayed these incredible instructions to the children of Israel, and they followed his orders without grumbling. After all, had they not passed over Jordan on dry land?

One can imagine the consternation of the natives of Jericho as they watched the strange spectacle of tens of thousands of men marching around their city. Thump! Thump! Thump! sounded the feet of those straggly-bearded men clothed in forty-year-old garments. None of the marchers said a word, and their silence made the thump, thump, thump of their feet even worse. For hours and hours the marching continued, and as it continued the thump, thump, thump became more regular. Soon the watchers were so thoroughly frightened, their hearts began to thump in rhythm to the feet of the men outside.

On the seventh day the marchers rounded the walls of Jericho seven times. Then, as they completed the seventh round, the horns were blown and Joshua signaled the people to shout. This was the moment everyone had been awaiting. Suddenly the hands of everyone—grandfathers, grandmothers, middle-aged people, newlyweds, teenagers, little children— were cupped to their mouths, and they shouted until their throats ached. And in the midst of their shouts, the wall fell down flat.

As the dust of the fallen walls filled the air, the warriors rushed into the city. The battle was over.

Joshua's men remembered the pledge made by the spies to Rahab and they spared her life and those of her relatives. What happened to Rahab? She, believe many researchers, became the wife of Salmon and eventually the mother of Boaz. Matthew lists her as an ancestor of Jesus (Matthew 1:5). And later, the author of the Book of Hebrews gave her a niche in his list of the faithful (Hebrews 11:31).

Joshua, too, finished his earthly life in an honorable and dis-

tinguished manner. The Septuagint has a record of his
burial.

> And after those things, Joshua the son of Naue,
> the servant of the Lord, died at the age of a hun-
> dred and ten years; and they buried him in the
> boundaries of his inheritance at Thamnasachar, on
> mount Ephraim, north of mount Gaas. There they
> deposited with him, in the grave in which they
> buried him, the stone knives with which he had cir-
> cumcised the children of Israel at Galgala, as the
> Lord commanded them, when he had brought them
> out of Egypt. And they are there at this day (Joshua
> 24:29-31).

Chapter 23

Gaza: City of Rebels

The city of Gaza, one of the most southern cities in Palestine, has many reasons to be visited—and remembered.

Our word gauze has roots in the name Gaza. Being only a scant three miles east of the Mediterranean, Gaza was an important post for caravans moving between Mesopotamia and Egypt. It was also a stronghold of the Philistines.

As a five-year-old, I had a great interest in Gaza. My interest centered on the fact that my hero Samson also loved Gaza. The story of the end of his life in Gaza: his imprisonment and his final destruction of the temple dedicated to the worship of Dagon, held me in a firm grip. But before we get into that, let's take a quick look at the birth and growth of this city which is even now a point of dispute in the Arab-Israeli conflict.

The first reference to Gaza in the Bible is in Genesis 10:19. "And the border of the Canaanites was from Sidon, as thou comest to Gerar, unto Gaza; as thou goest, unto Sodom, and Gomorrah. . . ."

Even in those days of Abraham—at least 2000 B.C.—Gaza was known for its Philistine connections. This fact has been disputed. *Britannica*, in its article on *Philistia* in the 14th edition, makes the dogmatic statement: "In Gen. 21:32-34 and Ex. 13:17; 15:14; 23:31 the references to Philistia are anachronistic."

In his comments on this, Gleason L. Archer has said: "The five main cities of the Philistines, or at least those that have been excavated, uniformly show occupation extending back to the Hyksos times and before . . . Inscribed seals found at Gaza bear the names of Twelfth Dynasty kings like Amenemhat III (1842 B.C.). Hence there can be no doubt that this area was occupied by strong kingdoms back in the patriarchal age. To be sure, their population may have been pre-Philistine, but there is absolutely no proof that such was the case" (*Encyclopedia of Bible Difficulties*).

The Tell el-Amarna correspondence (1400-1370 B.C.) shows that Gaza was, at that time, loyal to Egypt.

The children of Israel got a foothold in Gaza, but their control didn't last, for the Philistines were firmly entrenched. Joshua 13 outlines the problem. "Now Joshua was old and stricken in years; and the Lord said unto him . . . There remaineth yet very much land to be possessed. This is the land that yet remaineth: all the borders of the Philistines, and all Geshuri" (vss. 1-2). He then enumerated the five lords of the Philistines: "the Gazathites, and the Ashdothites, the Eshkalonites, the Gittites, and the Ekronites" (vs. 3).

Solomon's territory reached Gaza but it did not include it. And Amos denounced the city:

> Thus saith the Lord; For three transgressions of Gaza, and for four, I will not turn away the punishment thereof; because they carried away captive the whole captivity, to deliver them up to Edom. But I will send a fire on the wall of Gaza, which shall devour the palaces thereof (Amos 1:6-7).

These prophecies of Amos—786-746 B.C.—came to pass in an exceedingly dramatic way. Listen to Josephus: "When Alexander [the Great] saw that Ptolemy was retired from Gaza to Cyprus, and his mother Cleopatria was returned to Egypt, he grew angry at the people of Gaza because they had invited Ptolemy to assist them . . . As Apollodotus, the general of the army of Gaza, fell upon the camp of the Jews by night, with two thousand foreign and ten thousand of his own forces, while the night lasted, those of Gaza prevailed, because the enemy was made to believe that it was Ptolemy who attacked them; but when day was come on, and that mistake was corrected, and the Jews knew the truth of the matter, they came back again and fell on Gaza, and slew of them about a thousand. . . .

"Alexander, who, when he came in at first, lay quiet, but afterward set his army upon the inhabitants of Gaza, and gave them [his men] leave to punish them; so some went one way, and some went another, and slew the inhabitants of Gaza; yet were they not of cowardly hearts, but opposed those that came to slay them, and slew as many of the Jews; and some of them when they saw themselves deserted, burnt their own houses, that the enemy might get none of their spoils; nay, some of them, with their own hands, slew their children and their wives, having no other way but this of avoiding slavery for them . . ." (*Antiquities of the Jews*, Book XIII, Part 3).

More than two centuries after the years of Alexander the Great, the Romans became masters of Gaza during their conquest of Palestine. At that time, Gaza became famous as a place where pagan vices were practiced.

Gaza is only mentioned once in the New Testament. That was when the angel of the Lord directed Philip to go there. It was on this occasion that the Ethiopian eunuch was won over to the way of Christ, and this was the beginning of the evangelization of Ethiopia.

It was during the period of the judges that Samson fell into sin in Gaza. His exploits astounded me. I especially liked the way he killed the lion and how he escaped from Gaza. My eyes were always wide when the housekeeper who took care of me read how Samson escaped. At this dramatic point, she would lean slightly forward and read:

> And Samson lay till midnight, and arose at midnight, and took the doors of the gate of the city, and the two posts, and went away with them, bar and

197

> all, and put them upon his shoulders, and carried
> them up to the top of an hill that is before Hebron
> (Judges 16:3).

As I recall, she never explained that Hebron was thirty-eight miles away. That would have indeed captivated me, for that was ten times the distance to my father's church!

Ah, but my favorite episode concerned the way Samson teased Delilah about the source of his strength. First, he insisted that if he were bound with seven bowstrings he would be like other men. When Samson broke these "as a thread of tow is broken when it toucheth the fire" Delilah knew she had been deceived. Next, he told her that he should be bound with new ropes, then that his hair should be woven into a web. (The availability of a web indicates that this was, indeed, a cloth manufacturing center.) After the last version proved also to be false, Samson revealed the fact that his strength was in his hair.

The disaster that followed after Samson had had his locks cut pulled me onto the edge of my seat even though I could have quoted the story myself. Leaning forward I listened as "Auntie" read from the Bible:

> The Philistines took him, and put out his eyes,
> and brought him down to Gaza, and bound him
> with fetters of brass; and he did grind in the prison
> house (Judges 16:21).

Ah, but that wasn't the end! While Samson pushed the grindstone around and around, his hair continued to grow. First it reached his chin and then his shoulders. And "then the lords of the Philistines gathered . . . to offer a great sacrifice unto Dagon their god, and to rejoice: for they said, Our god hath delivered Samson our enemy into our hand . . . And it came to pass, when their hearts were merry, that they said, Call for Samson, that he may make us sport. And they called for Samson out of the prison house; and he made them sport: and they set him between the pillars ... Now the house was full of men and women; and all the lords of the Philistines were there; and there were upon the roof about three thousand men and women, that beheld while Samson made sport" (vss. 23-25,27).

While Samson was being ridiculed he felt the ends of his hair on his shoulders. Yes, it was getting long! But was it long enough? Well, he would pray to the God of Abraham, Isaac, and Jacob.

> And Samson called unto the Lord, and said, O Lord God, remember me, I pray thee, and strengthen me, I pray thee, only this once, O God, that I may be at once avenged of the Philistines for my two eyes (vs. 28).

Samson had been led to the two middle pillars which supported the roof. Now he placed his left arm around one and his right arm around the other. Then, from the depths of his heart, he groaned another prayer: "Let me die with the Philistines."

His head low, his arms around the pillars, Samson paused to fill his lungs with breath. A few feet away he could hear the laughter and small talk of the lords and their ladies. With effort, he shut them out. Then he applied his strength. Suddenly as he squeezed, he became conscious of new strength. Yes, the Lord was helping him. All at once, one of the pillars gave a little; and then the other moved a little more. Then they collapsed.

Judges 16:30 relates the end of the story.

> And the house fell upon the lords, and upon all the people that were therein. So the dead which he slew at his death were more than they which he slew in his life.

Yes, all of this took place in Gaza. Did Samson make the gallery of faith? Of course! Read Hebrews 11:32.

Chapter 24

Damascus:
World's Oldest City

Anyone with the courage to face a Damascene and deny that his city is the oldest city in the universe will be met with a shrug, a pitiful stare—and an articulate volley of legends.

"Abraham was the first king of Damascus!" declare many.

"You see," they explain, "Damascus was founded by Demshak. Demshak was a slave given to Abraham by no other than Nimrod, the great-grandson of Noah."

Others insist that Damascus is much, much older than Abraham. "This is the center of the Garden of Eden." And, if you don't believe it, they will take you to the bell-shaped tomb of Abel. The common belief is that Cain killed him in a mysterious place very close to the city.

Is Damascus really that old? It may not be the first city ever founded. That distinction probably belongs to Old Jericho. But it may well be the oldest continuously inhabited city in the world. Josephus wrote: "Shem, the third son of Noah, had five sons, who inhabited the land that began at Euphrates, and reached the Indian Ocean . . . Elam left behind him the Elamites, the ancestors of the Persians. Ashur lived at the city Nineveh; and named his subjects Assyrians . . . Arphaxed named the Arphaxadites, who are now called Chaldeans . . .

Aram had the Aramites, which the Greeks call Syrians . . . Of the four sons of Aram, Uz founded Trachonitis and Damascus: this country lies between Palestine and Celesyria. . ." (*Antiquities of the Jews*, Book I. Chapter VI. Part 4).

Is this statement of Josephus truth or legend? No one knows. But archaeologists have turned up hints that ancient men did live in this area thousands of years before Christ. The first Biblical mention is Genesis 14:15 where we are told that Abram pursued the enemy "unto Hobah, which is on the left hand of Damascus."

Damascus is mentioned forty-five times in the Old Testament.

Having performed my parents' 50th wedding anniversary in Nairobi in 1958, I found myself in Beirut, Lebanon with two days to spare. This meant one thing. I had to go to Damascus! Nonetheless, I was wary even though Damascus was less than sixty miles away. Two or three years prior to this, two of my friends had taken a taxi in Beirut and had gone to Damascus. There, they had become involved in the most terrifying experience of their lives. Each had related his story to me.

At the Syrian border the taxi driver had stopped at the proper place for my friends to get their Syrian visas. Since the clerk was not in his office, the driver said, "It's all right. Let's go on. We'll only be in Syria for a few hours. No one will know. It won't make any difference."

While the pair was standing on the Street Called Straight, their eyes became riveted onto a man who had just been legally hanged. His neck still in the noose, he was being wheeled down the street on a portable gallows. An oilcloth listing his crimes was suspended from his neck. As my friends stood breathlessly watching, a policeman accosted them. "Passports!" he demanded.

Since the men had no visas, they were promptly arrested, accused of being Jewish spies—and threatened with prison. Fortunately, their names were not Jewish, and after it had been noted in their passports that they were never to visit Syria again, they were released.

Fearing a similar experience, I arranged to make the trip with a Christian Lebanese. We duly stopped at the Syrian border. Again the clerk was missing. But we waited until I had a Syrian visa. Then we told the taxi driver to continue on to Damascus.

As we stood on the Street Called Straight—Suk et-Tawileh "The Long Street" in Arabic—my mind went back to Saul of Tarsus. Today the street runs in the northwest-southeast direction just as it did in his day. Likewise, its two-mile length and the straightness of its course is about the same. In other ways, however, it is quite different. During New Testament times the street was a wide, elaborate avenue flanked by Corinthian columns. Several hundred years later, the street was even more elaborate. "Sixteen hundred years ago, walls of hewn limestone, fifteen feet thick, rose along the banks of the Barada, and were buttressed by a *castrum* in the west. From the Gate of Jupiter to the Gate of the Sun ran the Street Called Straight . . . A forum had succeeded the agora. In the walls stood triple entrances, the gates of Saturn, Mars and the Moon, the temple of Venus and portals of Venus" (*Mirror to Damascus*, Thubron Colin).

Today, the street made famous by Paul runs through a rather poor section. That made no difference to me. I wanted to walk where Saul of Tarsus had walked, and I wanted to visit the house of Ananias where Saul recovered his sight.

The traditional house of Ananias is about fifteen steps below the surface of the street. There, on the Roman street level, I was shown what is considered to be the actual spot where the two opposites met. It is about thirty-five feet long; and, other than for a few pews and a table or two, completely bare.

To me, the only thing impressive about the place was the memory of how Saul had been received by a member of the group he had persecuted, and how he had emerged from his presence as a new man.

Back on the Street Called Straight, I entered a shop and asked to see some tablecloths. Having been raised in Kenya, I was used to haggling over price, and I considered myself an expert. But on this occasion there was no haggling. The storekeeper knew that an American tourist would gladly pay double price for an item purchased on the Street Called Straight!

There are forty-five references to Damascus in the Old Testament. David put garrisons in Damascus. Ben-hadad, Ahab's old enemy, lived in this city. It was also the home of Naaman the army commander who suffered from leprosy and who sought out the help of Elisha.

Isaiah didn't have a very high opinion of this ancient city. He prophesied: "The riches of Damascus and the spoil of Samaria shall be taken away before the king of Assyria" (Isaiah 8:4). Jeremiah, too, had a word to say about the city's future. "And I will kindle a fire in the wall of Damascus, and it shall consume the palaces of Ben-hadad" (Jeremiah 49:27).

These predictions came to pass. In 732 B.C. Damascus fell into the hands of Tiglath-pileser. Josephus provided insight into what happened. "Now this king [Tiglath-pileser]. . .came to assist Ahaz, and made war on the Syrians, and laid their country to waste, and took Damascus by force, and slew Rezin their king, and transported the people of Damascus into Upper Media, and brought a colony of Assyrians, and planted them in Damascus."

Centuries later, the Romans conquered Syria; and Mark Antony, being a generous man, presented Damascus, together with about half of Syria, to the flame of his heart— Cleopatra.

Damascus remains a remarkable city. At their Great Mosque I was shown the tomb of John the Baptist and was told that when Jesus Christ descends to earth at His Second Coming, His feet will first touch the minaret of this mosque.

On my way back to Beirut the taxi driver and my escort got into a long heated discussion. Since I do not speak Arabic, I was concerned about what was being said. Had I, too, been the victim of a conspiracy? But I need not have worried, for soon my escort muffled a nervous cough and said, "Brother Ludwig, I think it would be proper to pay the driver an extra five pounds."

That, I thought, was a satisfactory ending. I paid the five pounds and checked into my hotel.

Chapter 25

Alexandria: City of Lights

Alexandria, Egypt is not mentioned in the Old Testament, and it is only mentioned indirectly four times in the New Testament. Why, then, include a chapter about it in this section of the book concerned with Old Testament cities?

The answer is easy. Although Alexandria is not mentioned in the Old Testament, tradition says that a work was started there by seventy wise men and completed in seventy days which helped pave the way for the ministry of Jesus Christ and the evangelistic work of the apostles—especially that of the Apostle Paul.

Moreover, the light that was lit in Alexandria is another proof that the Lord often uses the wrath of men to praise Him. But to understand this we must learn how Alexandria came into being.

In 332 B.C. Alexander the Great decided that he should found a new city in Egypt and name it Alexandria. Inflamed by his dream of a great new city, he announced several projects. "It must have a lighthouse, and that lighthouse must be taller than the pyramids. Especially that of Cheops! Also, there must be a vast library where the works of Homer and others can be placed on display. In addition, there must be a magnificent temple—and gymnasium. People must learn! I am what I am because of Aristotle, Homer—and books."

Just before he left this section of Egypt, Alexander decided to mark the lines where the walls should be laid. Not having stakes, he used ground barley from his soldiers' rations. The barley flour made clear, white lines. But by the time he had finished, clouds of birds had descended from a nearby marsh and were devouring his carefully laid out plans.

Stunned by this terrible omen, Alexander summoned his soothsayers. "What does it mean?" he demanded.

His chief wise man Aristander didn't know what to answer. But after some thought, he said, "It means the city will prosper, but only from the harvests of the earth."

Alexander the Great died in Babylon in 323 B.C. But his dreams of building a great city remained—as did the projects he had outlined. At that time there were very few lighthouses on the coasts. Ship captains had to be content with landmarks, and these could not be seen at night; and so it was decided to build a magnificent lighthouse on the reef-encircled island of Pharos at the western side of Alexandria's harbor.

Sostratus, the Greek architect, had one major goal in mind. This lighthouse must be worthy of Alexander the Great! Legend has it that the tower was built of great blocks of hewn limestone and ornamented with an even whiter marble. The task took twenty years to complete. The cost totaled eight hundred talents. Since a talent was worth $40,000 at that time, the total cost was a staggering $32,000,000—an unbelievable sum in 280 B.C., the year it was completed.

No one knows how that lighthouse, known as "The Pharos," was lighted. The assumption is that ordinary firewood was burned at the top. This means that the inside winding ramp was constantly choked by carts overflowing with firewood. As to the effectiveness of the light there is no doubt. Pliny the Elder wrote: "The use of the watch-tower is to show as a lantern and give direction in the night season to ships." But he was worried that the light was so brilliant it could "appear unto the sailors in the manner of a star."

The base of the Pharos was square. It covered 10,000 square feet. The pinnacle was topped by the statue of Poseidon—the god of the seas. If these figures are correct, and some ancients make them larger, this lighthouse was the largest ever built.

The Pharos, one of the seven wonders of the world, guided ships for 1,600 years. It was leveled by an earthquake in A.D. 1375. The ruins were turned into both a mosque and a fort.

Without realizing it, however, Alexandria became the base for a group of men who produced a light far brighter than the Pharos. Moreover, that light is still shining. Here are the basic facts of that story.

Alexander the Great had determined that Greek culture would be spread around the world. It was because of this passion that he provided thousands of scholarships to the best universities in Greece. (See chapter 12.)

As nation after nation fell to Alexander's armies, Greek became a second language to those who had been conquered. The rabbis resented this intrusion of Greek. Nonetheless, in time, Greek spread everywhere. Those who wanted better jobs had to speak Greek. This fact is underlined by the many references to Greek in the New Testament.

During the reign of Ptolemy II Philadelphus, king of Egypt, the rabbis in Alexandria decided that their Hebrew Bible had to be translated into Greek so that their youth and the Greek-speaking world could read it. The story of how this was done has been related by Aristeas who claimed to be an eyewitness. Since scholars have shown that Aristeas made several gross mistakes, his story is suspect. Even so, it is extremely interesting!

According to Aristeas, this work was done by seventy-two scholars in seventy-two days. These men, who had to have lived "blameless lives," did their translating on the island of Pharos. Thus, they labored near the base of the famous lighthouse!

The reason seventy-two scholars were employed, explains Josephus, is because six were chosen from each tribe. At the conclusion of the work, it was so well received it was announced that a curse would be placed on anyone who made a single change.

This translation is known as the Septuagint, or the LXX (Roman numerals for 70). It was used by Greek-speaking Jews and Gentiles throughout the Mediterranean world. Jesus and the apostles were constantly using the words "as it is written." Those who wanted to check on their accuracy had access to either the Septuagint or Hebrew scrolls.

Had such men as Paul or Luke wanted to emphasize that Jesus was born of a virgin, they had immediate access to the Old Testament in either Greek or Hebrew. The English translation of the Septuagint's rendering of Isaiah 7:14 reads: "Therefore the Lord Himself will give you a sign: Behold, the virgin shall conceive and bear a son, and he shall be called *Emmanuel* [God-with-us]" (The Septuagint Bible. The Falcon's Wing Press).

Was the Septuagint translated by seventy scholars in seventy days or by seventy-two scholars in seventy-two days? That remains a point of debate. The Greek Septuagint is easily available in English. And it is a useful tool for all students of the Scripture.

In the early days of Christianity, before the Gospels and Epistles were generally available, the Septuagint was the resource used throughout the non-Hebrew speaking world. Thus it was a powerful beacon and guided many a congregation as the members checked on the words of their pastors.

In his *Cambridge Ancient History* (Vol. VI), W. W. Tarn made this comment about Alexander the Great: "He lifted the civilized world out of one groove and set it in another; he started a new epoch; nothing could again be as it had been."

True. But as blue-eyed Alexander waged war did he realize

that by spreading Greek around the world he was making it easier for the Good News of Jesus Christ to be effective in the world he knew so well? The answer to that is a definite no. Like Cyrus and Nebuchadnezzar, Alexander had made moves and had been used in mysterious ways which he did not understand.

Chapter 26

Jerusalem:
The Immovable City

Jerusalem has been destroyed and rebuilt several times. But, unlike Jericho, it has never been moved. This is intriguing, for, from a commercial point of view, it is not ideally located. Babylon and Nineveh straddled rivers which both supplied water and acted as ports. Jerusalem is not close to a river nor a port—and it is 33 miles from the Mediterranean. Moreover, Jerusalem was never a part of the caravan routes.

Considering its poor location, one would think that when Nehemiah rebuilt the walls, he would have chosen a better location. In our mind's eye, each of us can see Nehemiah as he rode around the remnants of the walls making his survey. Knowing that the king of Babylon was backing him, this was a great opportunity to rebuild the city on a port. But even though he was helped by men from Jericho who knew how their city had been moved, the thought of rebuilding Jerusalem in another area never entered his mind. Why?

While Jerusalem was never on a trade route, it has other assets. One of those assets is its altitude of 2550 feet. During the hot summers when the heat in nearby Jericho is nearly suffocating, Jerusalem is many degrees cooler. Indeed, the average temperature during the year is a comfortable 63 degrees.

Another asset is the series of Judean hills. They not only offered protection, but also shadows. Those shadows throw contrast and coolness across the city. As for water, the Gihon Spring—Gihon means *a bursting forth*—supplied all the water Old Testament Jerusalem needed. Because of these advantages, a psalmist wrote: "Beautiful for situation, the joy of the whole earth, is mount Zion, on the sides of the north, the city of the great King" (48:2).

Ah, but these physical attributes are not the only cause for the Jewish love of Jerusalem. Another reason was revealed by Nehemiah when he addressed the king. Said the cupbearer: "If it please the king, and if thy servant [has] found favor in thy sight, that thou wouldest send me unto Judah, unto the *city of my fathers' sepulchres*, that I may build it" (Nehemiah 2:5; italics mine).

Those words, "city of my fathers' sepulchres," indicate how close Jerusalem was to his heart. As a lad, growing up in Babylon, he had heard the stories about his forefathers again and again. Undoubtedly a favorite was about Abraham.

God had faithfully promised Abraham that he would be the "father of many nations" and yet his wife did not conceive. The years hurried by, but her arms remained empty. Then, when she was about 89 Sarah overheard the Angel tell her husband that she would have a son. Greatly amused, "Sarah laughed within herself." But as the Angel had promised, she did have a son. This son, heir of the promise, was named Isaac (Laughter). All went well, then the Lord spoke unto Abraham: "Take now thy son, thine only son Isaac, whom thou lovest, and get thee into the land of Moriah; and offer him there for a burnt-offering upon one of the mountains which I will tell thee of" (Genesis 22:2).

The Lord led Abraham to a place where the sacrifice was to be made; and then, at the last moment, provided a ram for the sacrifice. Jewish tradition insists that this incident took place on the Rock Moriah next to the threshing floor which David purchased from Ornan for "six hundred shekels of gold by weight" (I Chronicles 21:25).

All of this had taken place in Jerusalem!

In addition, there was the history about how the city had been acquired by David from the Jebusites through conquest. Every niche and corner in the city had its history and its appeal to every Jewish heart. Likewise, Jerusalem had been the home of many of the great prophets: Isaiah, Jeremiah, Zedekiah, Micah, Habakkuk, Zephaniah, Haggai, and Zechariah.

Old Testament Jerusalem has been called many things over the centuries. In the Egyptian "Execration Texts" dating back to the eighteenth and nineteenth centuries B.C. the name appears as *Urushalim*. In the days of Abraham it was Salem. In the el-Amarna letters it is referred to as Beth-shalem. In Psalm 76:2, it is referred to as Salem. The passage reads: "In Salem also is his tabernacle, and his dwelling place in Zion." The present name Jerusalem means "Foundation of Salem."

Since New Testament times the name of Jerusalem has been changed twice. First by the Roman Emperor Hadrian who rebuilt the city (after its destruction in A.D. 70) and renamed it Aelia Capitolina in A.D. 135. Then, in A.D. 687 the Moslems took the city and renamed it Al-Quds. But through it all, the name Jerusalem has persisted.

Old Jerusalem had many walls. Many of these have been discovered and drawn on maps. But others have not and this causes a problem for archaeologists have not been able to make excavations at certain places and thus locate and date certain walls. The reason for this is that the owners of the land are reluctant to grant the necessary permission.

Because of this, scholars have to shrug about uncharted walls. Just where was the First North Wall? No one can be absolutely certain. This uncertainty has kept scholars from being completely assured about the place where Jesus was crucified and buried.

Many claim that the exact spot is marked by the location of

the Church of the Holy Sepulchre. Others say, no, this could not be, for Hebrews 13:12 tells us that He "suffered without the gate." And since the Church of the Holy Sepulchre is definitely *inside* the gate, people have wondered.

Could Bishop Macarius have been mistaken when he identified the spot in A.D. 326? As a bishop, he certainly knew what the writer of Hebrews said! Ah, but maybe if that North Wall could be located it would show that the Church of the Holy Sepulchre was on the other side of that wall.

The popular place to visit the Empty Tomb is now the so-called Garden Tomb, and this tomb plus the nearby skull-shaped cliffs meets the requirements of many of the passages in the New Testament. To make certain, whenever I'm in Jerusalem I visit both places; although, I must admit, I spend more time at the Garden Tomb!

Altogether three temples were built in Jerusalem. That of Solomon; then that of Zerubbabel which was completed in 516 B.C. (This was so small Jews do not count it.) And finally that of Herod the Great which was started between 20 and 19 B.C.

Many tourists to Jerusalem are disappointed when they learn that the present walls date to Suleiman the Magnificent who had them built around A.D. 1542. This should not be too great a disappointment for, after all, the walls *were* rebuilt—and Jerusalem was *not* moved. Moreover, Herod's Western Wall remains.

Nineveh straddled a river; but that river moved, and Nineveh is gone. Babylon straddled a river, but that river moved, and Babylon is gone. Jerusalem, however, was built by a perpetual spring, and Jerusalem remains!

Appendixes

Appendix A

Old Testament Chronology

Old Testament chronology is not as simple as some distinguished Christian scholars once assumed. In the 1650s, James Ussher, arch-bishop of Armagh in northern Ireland, wrote that Creation Week started on the evening of October 22, 4004 B.C. He was not the first to determine such a precise date. Several years before, John Lightfoot, noted Greek scholar and vice-chancellor of Cambridge University, had been even more precise. Without blinking, he stated that Adam took his first breath on Friday, 3928 B.C. at 9:00 A.M.!

These brilliant gentlemen meant well. Their problem was that they did not have access to the discoveries of modern archaeology, nor had cuneiform or hieroglyphics been deciphered.

The immense difficulties we have in Old Testament chronology are pointed out by a difficulty we have in our own time. According to the latest calendar, George Washington was born on February 22, 1732. Strictly speaking, however, he was born on February 11. Why the difference? Because the Gregorian Calendar—the one now in use—was adopted when George Washington was quite young. That calendar shortened 1732 by eleven days. (The Julian calendar, which had been in effect since Julius Caesar, was corrected by Pope Gregory in 1582, but the correction was not adopted by England and her colonies until 1752.)

Another example of the problems facing chroniclers is that of the year in which Christ was born. Today, we know that when Dennis the Little divided the centuries into A.D. and B.C. about 525 A.D., he made a mistake of at least four years. Thus, it is estimated that Jesus was born between 4 and 7 B.C. This fact is accepted by most people.

Old Testament chronology has even more problems. Let's glance at a few.

The Bible Almanac states: "After the death of King Solomon and the division of the kingdom, it seems the chroniclers in the southern kingdom of Judah counted the official reign of their kings from the Hebrew month of Ethanim, or Tishri (September-October)—the beginning of the civil year. In the northern kingdom of Israel, scribes used the month of Abib, or Nisan (March-April)—the beginning of the religious year."

Across the centuries and many kings, that much difference could be quite large.

Another problem is that all ancient historians were not consistent. One king might be listed as having reigned from a certain year when, as a matter of fact, he only reigned for one month during that year. Other kings did not count that first month or six months. In their system only full years counted. A parallel of this problem is in the manner in which we count our ages. According to some Europeans, we are a year old when we are born. And, in a way, that is correct! Confronted with this problem, scholars have to decide how the years in a certain reign were counted. Fortunately, this is often possible.

An additional difficulty revolves around genealogy. In the Bible a prominent character is sometimes listed as the father of another when actually he is only a distant paternal relative. This occurs in Matthew 1:8. There, the writer infers that Jehoram was the father of Uzziah. (Note the variation in Matthew's spelling.) Actually, Jehoram was the great, great grandfather of Uzziah!

Does this mean that Matthew was mistaken? Certainly not. His readers knew what he was saying, for he simply used a method with which they were acquainted.

Old Testament chronology is difficult. However, thanks to murals, astronomy, and ancient records, some dates can be pinpointed. For example, Josephus informed us in his *Antiquities* that an eclipse of the moon preceded the death of

Herod the Great (Book XVII. Chapter XIII, Section 2). Astronomers assure us that there were three eclipses in 5 and 4 B.C. Of these, scholars are convinced that the one most probably before Herod's death was that of March 12, 4 B.C. Assured of this date, the fact that Jesus was born from 4 to 7 B.C. is confirmed, for Herod the Great was alive at the time of Jesus' birth.

Scholars who have given their lives to the study of Biblical chronology have come up with an amazing assortment of tools to make their determinations. And, although they disagree among themselves, they have achieved many extremely well documented guesses.

Believing that viewing Bible characters and cities in juxtaposition with contemporary events of the times helps to put new dimensions into those characters and events, we have prepared the following chart.

Bible Characters and Cities
Viewed with Contemporary Events

B.C.	Biblical	Contemporary

The World of Abraham

It should be kept in mind that Abraham was born into a very cultured world. Copper, bronze, iron, gold and silver had come into use. Sailboats had been developed and the Egyptians were sailing the Mediterranean. The wheel had been invented in Sumer. The horse was domesticated, and such farm implements as plows were in use in the Near East. The Egyptian calendar had been devised and pyramids built in Egypt. Writing was well-developed in various forms: Egyptian hieroglyphics, Babylonian cuneiform, and some alphabetic writing discovered in mines in the south Sinai has been dated by some scholars to the period before Abraham. A large roster of pagan gods were worshiped in all parts of the known world.

B.C.	Biblical	Contemporary
2166	Birth of Abraham	
2091	Call of Abraham	
2000		Chicken and elephant domesticated in India.
1876	Joseph sold as slave. Later becomes Egyptian official.	

1750		Laws of Hammurabi compiled (?).
1700		Hyksos use chariots in Egypt.
1570		Hyksos driven out of Egypt.
1528 (?)		Birth of Hatshepsut, daughter of Thutmose I.
1526 (?)	Birth of Moses	Ruling pharaoh: Thutmose I. Out-rigger canoes were being used in the South Pacific.
1504		Death of Thutmose II.
1486	Moses kills Egyptian and flees to land of Midianites	
1446	The Exodus	Thutmose III died 1450. His son Amenhotep was in power at the time of Moses' negotiations. (This point is subject to sharp debate).
1406	Death of Moses. Joshua leads Israel into Canaan.	Alphabet is devised in Ugarit.
1400 (?)	Period of Judges begins. See appendix.	

1043	Saul is anointed king of Israel.	Phoenicians spread use of alphabet.
1011	David is crowned king of Judah.	
1004	David becomes king of all 12 tribes.	
971	Solomon becomes third king of all Israel.	
967	Construction of Solomon's Temple begins. It took seven and a half years to complete it.	
931	Death of Solomon. His kingdom divides. Kings for each side listed in appendix.	
753		Mythical founding of Rome.
612	Fall of Nineveh.	Medes, Babylonians, and Scythians plunder Nineveh.
605		Nebuchadnezzar ascends throne of Babylon.

606	Nebuchadnezzar imprisons Jehoiakim. Takes Daniel and Temple vessels to Babylon.	
597	Nebuchadnezzar returns to Jerusalem. Takes 10,000 more prisoners and additional Temple vessels.	
	Jeremiah prophesies that the "exile" will last seventy years.	
586	Nebuchadnezzar returns to Jerusalem. Blinds Zedekiah. Takes 832 captives.	
555		Cyrus comes to power in Persia.
539	Babylon is conquered by Cyrus. Cyrus issued decree allowing Jews in captivity	

to return to
their homes.

From the 606
beginning of
exile to the de-
cree of Cyrus
was 67 years.
Jeremiah's
prophecy had
been fulfilled.
Even more re-
markable, Isaiah
had indicated
that Cyrus was
God's shepherd
about a century
and a half be-
fore his decree.

521	Darius begins reign in Persia.
509	Rome becomes a republic.
	Chinese invent wheelbarrow.
334	Alexander the Great crosses the Hellespont.
323	Alexander the Great dies in Babylon.

300		Symbol for zero invented.
168	Antiochus Epi-phanes desecra-tes Temple by sacrificing swine on the altar.	Waterwheel invented and comes into general use in the Near East.
165	Maccabean re-volt	
143	Simon, descen-dant of the Mac-cabees becomes high priest and ethnarch.	Alexandrian Jews adopt *koine* Greek as their language.
63	Judea falls to the Romans.	
31		As the result of the battle of Actium, Egypt comes under the rule of Rome.
27		Augustus Caesar comes to power as Rome's first emperor.
10 (?)	Birth of Saul of Tarsus	
4 (?)	Birth of Jesus	

Appendix B

JUDGES

The exact period of the Judges is extremely hard to determine. Even Paul had a problem! Luke quotes him as saying: "And after that he gave unto them judges *about* the space of four hundred and fifty years" (Acts 13:20; italics mine).

The problem is complicated by several difficulties: (1) We know that Joshua lived to be 110 years of age; but we do not know the year of his death (Joshua 24:29). Also, we know that Joshua's rule was followed by that of the elders (Joshua 24:31). (2) We do not know the precise tenure of each judge. (3) We can only guess at the number of years in which, due to apostasy, there was no judge. (4) Also, we have to wonder if some of the terms overlapped and some may have been localized. Nonetheless, here is a list of the judges and the reference that tells about each.

Othniel	Judges 3:7-11
Ehud	3:20
Barak and Deborah	4, 5
Gideon	6:1—8:32
Abimelech	8:33—9:57
Tola	10:1-2
Jair	10:3-5
Jephthah	11:1—12:7
Ibzan	12:8-10
Elon	12:11-12
Abdon	12:13-15
Samson	13:24—16:31

Finally, of course, we have Samuel who was a prophet as well as a judge, and who ended the period of the judges by anointing Saul king of Israel in 1043.

Appendix C

KINGS OF ISRAEL

KING	MEANING OF NAME(?)	CHARACTER	REIGN	MANNER OF DEATH
Jeroboam I	The people increases	Vile	22 yrs.	Natural
Nadab	God is liberal	Vile	3 yrs.	Murdered by Baasha
Baasha	The sun is Baal	Vile	24 yrs.	Natural
Elah	?	Vile	2 yrs.	Murdered while drunk by Zimri
Zimri	Pertaining to an antelope	Vile	7 days	Burned to death in his own palace which he set on fire
Omri	?	Horrible	12 yrs.	Natural
Ahab	Father's brother	The Worst	22 yrs.	Killed in battle
Ahaziah	Jehovah has seized	Vile	2 yrs.	Fell out of palace window

Joram	Jehovah is high	Mostly vile	12 yrs.	Jehu shot him through the heart with an arrow
Jehu	Jehovah is He	Mostly vile	28 yrs.	Natural
Jehoahaz	Jehovah has laid hold of	Vile	17 yrs.	Natural
Joash	Jehovah has given	Vile	16 yrs.	Murdered
Jeroboam II	The people increases	Vile	41 yrs.	Natural
Zechariah	Jehovah hath remembered	Vile	6 mo's.	Murdered
Shallum	Recompense	Vile	1 mo.	Murdered
Menahem	Comforter	Vile	10 yrs.	Natural
Pekahiah	Jehovah opens	Vile	2 yrs.	Murdered
Pekah	(God) has opened (the eyes).	Vile	20 yrs.	Murdered
Hoshea	Save	Vile	9 yrs.	Killed (?)

Appendix D

KINGS OF JUDAH

KING	MEANING OF NAME(?)	CHARACTER	REIGN	MANNER OF DEATH
Rehoboam	The people is enlarged	Mostly vile	17 yrs.	Natural
Abijah	Jehovah is a father	Mostly vile	3 yrs.	Natural
Asa	Physician	Good	41 yrs.	Natural
Jehoshaphat	Jehovah has judged	Excellent	25 yrs.	Natural
Jehoram	Jehovah is high	Vile	8 yrs.	Natural
Ahaziah	Jehovah has seized	Vile	1 yr.	Murdered
Athaliah*	Jehovah is exalted	Utterly vile	6 yrs.	Murdered
Joash	Jehovah has given	Good	40 yrs.	Murdered
Amaziah	Jehovah is strong	Good	29 yrs.	Murdered

Uzziah	Jehovah is strength	Good	52 yrs.	Died of leprosy
Jotham	Jehovah is perfect	Good	16 yrs.	Natural
Ahaz	Jehovah has seized	Vile	16 yrs.	Natural
Hezekiah	Jehovah is strength	Excellent	29 yrs.	Natural
Manasseh	Making to forget	Vile	55 yrs.	Natural
Amon	Faithful	Utterly vile	2 yrs.	Murdered
Josiah	Jehovah heals	Excellent	31 yrs.	Natural
Jehoahaz	Jehovah has laid hold of	Vile	3 mo's.	Murdered
Jehoiakim	Jehovah raises up	Vile	11 yrs.	Murdered
Jehoiachin	Jehovah establishes	Vile	3 mo's.	Natural
Zedekiah	Jehovah is righteous	Vile	11 yrs.	Died in prison

*Daughter of Ahab and Jezebel, she was actually a queen.

Selected Bibliography

The following books are among those that I found especially useful. Each is highly recommended.

Aldred, Cyril   *Tutankhamun's Egypt*, Charles Scribner's Sons, 1972.

Archer, Gleason L.   *Bible Difficulties*, Zondervan, 1982

Avi-Yonah, Michael   *Ancient Scrolls*, Lerner Publications, 1974

Bartlett, John R.   *Jericho*, Eerdman's Publishing Company, 1982

Blaiklock, E.M.   *The Zondervan Pictorial Atlas*, Zondervan, 1969.

Breasted, James H.   *Ancient Records of Egypt*, Vol. 1-5, Reissued by Russell and Russell, 1962.

British Museum, Trustees   *An Introduction to Ancient Egypt*, British Museum, 1979.

Colin, Thubron W.   *Mirror to Damascus*, William Heinemann, Ltd. 1967.

Contenau, Georges   *Everyday Life in Babylon and Assyria*, St. Martin's Press, 1954.

Cottrell, Leonard   *Lady of the Two Lands*, Bobbs-Merrill Co., 1967.

Cottrell, Leonard   *Land of Two Rivers*, World Publishing Company, 1962.

Cottrell, Leonard   *Life Under the Pharaohs*, Holt, Rinehart and Winston, 1961.

Cottrell, Leonard   *Egypt*, Nicholas Vane, 1966.

Cottrell, Leonard   *The Warrior Pharaohs*, Evans Brother, Ltd., London, 1968.

Daugherty, Raymond Philip   *Nabonidas and Belshazzar*, Yale University, 1929.

David, Rosalie   *Mysteries of the Mummies*, Cassell, Ltd., 1978.

Davis, John D.   *The Westminster Dictionary of the Bible*, Westminster Press, 1944.

Donovan, Frank   *Prepare Now for a Metric Future*, Weybright and Talley, 1970

Driver, G.R. and Miles, John C.   *The Babylonian Laws* (Legal Commentary), Oxford University Press, 1952.

Driver, G.R. and Miles, John C.   *The Babylonian Laws*, Oxford University Press, 1955.

Durant, Will   *The Life of Greece*, Simon and Schuster, 1939.

Edwards, Chilperic   *The Hammurabic Code*, Watts & Co., London, 1904.

Eilson, Robert Forest *The Living Pageant of the Nile*, Bobbs-Merrill Company, 1924.

Encyclopedia Britannica, 15th Edition, Encyclopedia Britannica, 1979.

Fagan, Bryan M. *Return to Babylon*, Little, Brown and Co., 1979.

Fakhry, Ahmed *The Pyramids*, University of Chicago Press, 1961.

Golding, Louis *In the Steps of Moses*, The Jewish Publication Society of America, 1943.

Habachi, Labib *The Obelisks of Egypt*, Charles Scribner's Sons, 1977.

Halley, Henry H. *Bible Handbook*, Zondervan, 1962.

Harris, James E. *X-raying Atlas of the Royal Mummies*, University of Chicago Press, 1980.

Harris, James E. *X-raying the Pharaohs*, Charles Scribner's Sons, 1973.

Hicks, Jim *The Persians*, Time-Life Books, 1975.

Herodotus Herodotus (Translated by George Rawlinson), Tudor Publishing Company, Copyright by Dial Press, 1928.

Hurry, Jamieson B. Oxford University Press, 1928.

Interpreter's Dictionary of the Bible, Abingdon Press, 1962.

Irwin, Keith Gordon *The Romance of Writing*, The Viking Press, 1956.

James, Fleming *Personalities of the Old Testament*, Charles Scribner's Sons, 1939.

Josephus, Flavius Holt, Rinehart and Winston.

Keller, Werner *The Bible as History*, William Morrow and Co., 1956.

Kenyon, Sir Frederic *The Bible and Archaeology*, Harper and Row, 1940.

Kenyon, Kathleen *Royal Cities of the Old Testament*, Schocken Books, Inc., 1971.

Kubie, Nora Benjamin *Road to Nineveh*, Doubleday Doran, 1964.

Lamb, Harold *Alexander of Macedon*, Doubleday & Company, 1946.

Ludwig, Emil *The Nile: the Life Story of a River*, Garden City, 1939.

Marlowe, John *The Golden Age of Alexandria*, Victor Gollanz, Ltd., 1971.

Mellersh, H.E.L. *Sumer and Babylon*, Thomas Crowell, 1965.

Miller, Madeleine S. and Lane, J. *Harper's Bible Dictionary*, Harper and Row, 1958.

Index

A

Abednego, 95-97, 168
Abel, 70, 200
Abishag, 65
abortion, 175
Abraham, 31, 35-36, 58,
    139-147, 178-180, 184, 200
Absalom, 63, 76
Abukir, 17
Acabus, 26
Accadia, 167
Achilles, 114
Adam, 70
Adonijah, 63-66
Aelia Capitolina, 212
Agamemnon, 117
Ahab, 82-85, 88
Ahaz, Achaz, 78, 81, 203
Ahaziah, king of Israel, 85-86
Ahaziah, king of Judah, 86-88
Ahijah, 76
Ahmhose, 49
Ahmose, 53
Akkad, 31-32
Alexander the Great, 110-119,
    123, 177, 196-197, 205-209
Alexandria, 17, 119, 205-209
Al-Hillah, 168
Al Quds, 212
Amarna Letters, 58
Amenemhat III, 196
Amenhotep I, 48-50
Amenhotep II, 59-61
Amenophis II, 59
Amorite, 33
Amos, 184, 196

Amraphel, 31-32, 36
Amun-Re, 19
Amyntas II, 113
Ananias, 202
Annu, 53
Antioch, Pisidia, 124
Antioch, Syria, 124, 126
Antiochus I (Soter), 124
Antiochus IV (Epiphanes),
    124-129
Antipater, 116
Apiru, 59
Apostles, The, 205
apple, 149
aqueduct, 150
Aram, Aramites, 201
Archer, Gleason L. 188, 196
Aristander, 206
Aristotle, 114, 205
ark, 14-15
Ark of the Covenant, 71, 185, 190
Arphaxad, Arphaxadites, 200
Artaxerxes, Mnemon, 30
Ashdodites, 196
Ashur, 200
Ashurbanipal, 153, 168
Asia, 117
Assyria, 16, 149-150, 153-154,
    167, 200, 203
astrologers, 105
astronomy, 26
Astyages, 108-109
Aswan, 165
Athaliah, 83
Azariah, 94

B

ba, 22
Baasha, 77
Babylon, 33, 81, 91-95, 97,
  100-103, 106, 109, 121,
  167-177, 210, 213
Babylonia, Babylonians, 32,
  91, 97, 151, 176
Baghdad, 168
barbarian, 133
barley, 149, 206
Barsine, 120
Basra, 139, 142
Bathsheba, 64-65
bean, 149
Behistun, 13
Beirut, Lebanon, 201, 204
Bel, 168
Belshazzar, 30, 101-102, 104,
  106-107, 176
Belteshazzar, 95
Ben-hadad, 203
Benjamin, tribe of, 184
Bethel, 183-186
Beth-shalem, 212
Birch, Samuel, 14
birds, 206
bittern, 151
Black Sea, 151
Boaz, 193
Bonaparte era, 46
book, 138, 205
Bouchard, General, 18
brass, 71,
brick, 158, 168, 170, 172
British Museum, 14, 16, 91,
  104, 139, 142-143, 152,
  154-155
bronze, 71
Bucephalus, 112-113, 117
bull, 170
burning bush, 59, 166
business, 173

Byron, Lord, 79

C

Caesar, Tiberius, 23
Cain, 70, 130, 200
Cairo Archaeological Museum,
  47, 60
cake, 164
Calah, 153
calendar, 26
Cambyses, 108
camel, 134
Canaan, Canaanite(s), 58-59,
  178, 183-186
canal, 132, 150
caravan, 134, 195, 210
Cary, H. F., 17
Celesyria, 201
Chaldeans, 105, 107, 200
Champollion, Jean Francois, 18
Chardin, Jean, 11
chariots, 39, 134, 150,
  163-164, 168
Cheops, 17, 20, 24, 205
cherry, 149
Christianity, 112, 122, 208
Church of the Holy Sepulchre,
  213
Cilician Gates, 135
circumcised, circumcision, 40,
  123, 127, 191
cities, 136
civilization, 30, 32
clay tablets, 136
Cleitus, 116, 120
Clement of Alexandria, 10
Cleopatra, 203
Cleopatria, 115, 196
Clothing, 144
code, Hammurabi's, 31, 33-37
Colin, Thurbron, 202
communication, 136

237

P

R

S

T